"For anyone embarking on a product management career, *Power Up Product Management* is a gem. Taylor and Naunheimer provide an engaging and practical guide to navigate your first 90 days with confidence. It's packed with actionable advice I wish I had when I was a wee little lad starting in product management."

—*Joff Redfern, Partner Menlo Ventures, ex-CPO Atlassian*

"To be a product manager is to learn, and I've done just that through every page of this guide.

As a new graduate in PM, I've been able to apply concepts — and more importantly, mental models — the book's in my day-to-day work.

"To be a product manager is to learn, and I've done just that through every page of this guide. As a new graduate in PM, I've been able to apply the book's concepts — and more importantly, mental models — in my day-to-day work. It is one of the only guides that captures all facets/core principles of being a Product Manager, which is especially important in a rapidly changing, AI-evolving time. This guide would be incredibly instrumental for students and anyone interested in succeeding in product management."

—*Austin Ma, Product at Microsoft*

"Having led over 25 product management teams throughout my career, it's clear this content can accelerate onboarding new talent from anywhere in the world, and it also supports leadership teams as we operationalize our problem-solving dreams into well-established products and solutions. I also appreciate the book's commentary on ethics in AI and will highly recommend the book to all of my colleagues in our AI development domain."

—*Jari Salomaa, CEO, former ServiceNow, Salesforce & Nokia product management leader*

"An outstanding primer on product management, providing a comprehensive guide to help anyone become an effective product manager. Taylor and Naunheimer offer invaluable perspectives and tools that equip both new and seasoned product managers to navigate constraints during product development and, most importantly, to create true product value."

—Tawanda Mahachi Director, Founder Institute Boston
and early stage startup advisor

"This book really helps give structure when there is often so much ambiguity to Product Management. If you followed every step of this guide, the end product would be a complete, customer-first solution, with every aspect thought through and robust road map forward. Even for seasoned PMs, I would recommend the guide for starting product management at a new company. Every company does it differently. Take a page out of this guide to put yourself on the right track."

—Samantha Spano, Senior Product Marketing
Manager, Salesforce

"It's to-the-point and very useful."

—Morgan Taylor-Cohen, UCLA Alum

"Walking into the world of product management, the first 90 days can make or break your new role. That's where Allison and Chris come in, offering newbies a lifeline with their book — it's like the Swiss Army Knife for product managers, but instead of blades and scissors, it's packed with the fundamental 'whys' of the trade. It's easy to get lost in the maze of New Product Introduction checklists that seem to forget the 'why'— but not with this guide. It's a compass, filtering out the noise and zooming in on what truly matters in product development. I cannot wait to see the next generation of products that are not just driven by customer needs but are defined by them."

—Susan Peterson Sturm, Cybersecurity Business Development
& Strategic Partnerships, Wabtec Corporation, 5x product
manager incl. Honeywell & GE and former GM ABB Digital

"Great information. A really good book. Incredibly useful. I could identify myself in the vignettes and loved reading them. The first few months are so hard, but it's a totally different experience with a resource like this.

I really liked many of the suggestions because they apply to so many aspects of the job, from writing product definitions, and even before determining the product itself."

—Nathalia Paulino, Product Marketing Manager

"Product managers come from many different backgrounds, and this book brings everyone together on the same page to effectively deliver solutions. We used it not only for coaching our new product talent, but also for our leadership team alignment and growth."

—Cesar David Salazar, Chief Operations Officer, Claro Enterprise Solutions

"This book helps Product Marketing people as well as Product Managers, especially when we work so closely together. Love the real-life scenarios. These gave me a clearer idea how strategy has to be implemented and how to improve go-to-market."

—Domenica Del Cioppo, Product Marketing Manager, Claro Enterprise Solutions

Power Up
Product Management

Power Up Product Management: A Quick Start Guide delivers a compact guide with expert guidance, tools, and exercises that empower new product managers to excel in their first weeks in their new position. Learn what it takes to build and sell outstanding products, how to define product value to impact product success, and why real-world product managers have failed or succeeded in gaining market traction.

The first in a series, this book helps anyone new to product go-to-market to quickly understand the overall product management function, including common product development methodologies, the criticality of "voice of customer," product stage definitions, and other PM essentials. The authors bring over 20 years of experience delivering software and hardware products globally for Fortune 500 companies and high-tech start-ups. Insights are delivered through real-life PM vignettes and to-the-point structured sections, making the quick start guide practical for both working PMs and new grads, or those considering a future PM or go-to-market career path. Executive leadership also benefits from the curated view into product management, which helps to develop a shared organizational-wide vision to guide improvements in people, process, and technology.

The book fills a gap in the market as an essential job companion with a fresh combination of knowledge, fun, and hands-on exercises to rapidly upskill or cross-skill in one of the most in-demand job areas today.

Power Up
Product Management
A Quick Start Guide

Allison J. Taylor and Chris Naunheimer

Routledge
Taylor & Francis Group
A PRODUCTIVITY PRESS BOOK

First published 2025
by Routledge
605 Third Avenue, New York, NY 10158

and by Routledge
4 Park Square, Milton Park, Abingdon, Oxon, OX14 4RN
Routledge is an imprint of the Taylor & Francis Group, an informa business

ISBN: 9781032950259 (hbk)
ISBN: 9781032939520 (pbk)
ISBN: 9781003582892 (ebk)

DOI: 10.4324/9781003582892

Typeset in Garamond
by Deanta Global Publishing Services, Chennai, India

On a Personal Note

Our families, who believe in us, light us up, and motivate us to perpetually learn and grow while still loving us for who we humanly are...to them we give our most intimate love and appreciation. You know who you are! This includes the next generation of product managers, designers, consultants, and collaborative innovators represented by our daughters, **Lauren Naunheimer** and **Morgan Taylor-Cohen**, who read this book as real readers and became an important part of its legacy.

Contents

Acknowledgments

Our sincere gratitude goes to our clients and organizations for trusting us with their humans and allowing us weekends, holidays, and evenings to give back to our communities through this book.

We also thank our many clients and students for their generous shares and intriguing feedback. This includes over a decade's worth of Thought Marketing clients that Allison has worked with, and the dozens of cohorts Chris has taught at Northwestern University. The representation across age, race, gender, life experiences, and nationalities speaks to the thrilling global and diverse interest in creating exceptional products!

Sherri Douville, powerhouse mentor and trailblazer at Medigram, originally kept the intellectual flashlight on through the caves of COVID as we published the first Routledge, Taylor & Francis title, *Mobile Medicine*. She then generously, graciously developed this opportunity for us to publish. She also lived by example, showing how diverse cross-functional teams deliver. Her Trustworthy Technology series with Routledge, Taylor & Francis, continues to inspire.

Our organizing editor, Kaara Kallen, chiropractically aligned our first content haul. Caroline Drakeley provided regular reviews that improved quality and loyally kept us on track. Longtime friend and skilled New York – now Portland book designer Kris Tobiassen generously advised on creative. The wise and experienced Kristine Mednansky escorted us through the hallowed halls of Routledge editorial processes.

Our product management communities contributed insights and encouragement to realize this work:

- Product managers: Dee Kimata (Schneider), Lisa Leiben, Rod Locke (Fortinet), Austin Ma (Microsoft), Kelly Rein (Honeywell), Sam Spano (Salesforce)
- Product marketing managers: Domenica Del Cioppo (Claro Enterprise Solutions), Nathalia Paulino, Kathy Trahan
- Innovators in our technology start-up world: Sara Drakeley (MobileCoin), Tawanda Mahachi (Founder Institute Boston)
- Academic researchers: Dr. Subin Im (Gary W. Rollins College of Business University of Tennessee at Chattanooga)
- Community PMs: Saeed Khan, PM consultant, Canada
- Product leadership: Eric Knapp (Opswat), Adrianna Peri and Cesar David Salazar (Claro Enterprise Solutions), Susan Peterson-Sturm (Wabtec), Dr. Joshua Tamayo-Sarver
- Early-stage reviewers included many of the above, as well as Olja Divas

About the Authors

Allison J. Taylor is a Silicon Valley technology go-to-market strategist and entrepreneur who has brought over 20 enterprise software solutions and services to market across 35 countries, representing over $3 billion in revenue. She founded her first company internationally at age 24 and is a former Middle East journalist and New York City medical trade press editor. An award-winning cybersecurity veteran, Allison consults senior leadership and their diverse cross-generational teams on growth and transformation strategies as founder and CEO of consulting firm Thought Marketing. She is also a co-founder of AI tech start-up company, Discerna. Allison's clients have included Honeywell, EMC/Dell, GE in addition to many early and mid-stage SaaS, cybersecurity and cloud start-ups worldwide. Her ample operating experience brings a dynamic practitioner view to her

Allison J. Taylor
Los Altos, CA
Linkedin.com/in/
allison-j-taylor-190219
Photo Credit:
Colleen Taylor-Hawk

knowledge, including cybersecurity product leadership positions at McAfee and Nokia, strategist roles at Sun Microsystems (now Oracle), and corporate communications leadership at legendary cybersecurity pioneer Check Point Software. She has coauthored two Routledge, Taylor & Francis books, with a third on the way for Artificial Intelligence (AI) & Cybersecurity, in close collaboration with a global cross-discipline team of experts in law, medicine, and engineering. Allison can be described as an "energy bomb," passionate about leaving the world a better place through well-designed technology solutions that benefit the human condition. She speaks multiple languages and holds an M.S. from San Jose State University (technology diffusion among software developers) and a B.A. in Spanish and Journalism from the University of Richmond, Virginia, in addition to many domain-specific certifications.

Chris Naunheimer has more than 30 years of experience at multinational Fortune 500 industrial companies with leadership roles in engineering, R&D, strategic planning, new product ventures, and user-centered design. He also is an adjunct faculty member and a former capstone project advisor at Northwestern University in the

Christopher Naunheimer
Greater Chicago Metro Area, Illinois
Linkedin.com/in/chrisnaunheimer/

Masters of Product Design and Development Management program. Over his career, Chris has been named inventor on 25 granted US utility patents and brings this innovation and continuous improvement mindset to his work. Coupled with his user experience design education and industry experience, this mindset brings a broad cross-functional skill set to his roles in industry and education. Chris is passionate about design and has a deeply held belief that we can use design to develop insights and solutions that can change people, cultures, and the world. He holds an M.S. in Product Design and Development Management from Northwestern University, Evanston, Illinois, and a B.S. in Mechanical Engineering, University of Illinois, Urbana-Champaign, Illinois.

Preface

Let Us Explain

Why Did We Write This Book?

After launching millions of dollars of products and working with a diverse range of product managers, we realized that many humans learn better when they have another human's insights, together with the latest tools.[1] A thoughtfully organized content package that a human can flip through can yield greater productivity, not to mention, a much-needed calming sense of control.

We also know, having coached hundreds of individuals, that it's hard to know what to do when, and why. Yes, you can scan information fragments online. Or take a months-long course. You can even ask the latest artificial intelligence tool. But how can you grasp the entirety of your first 90 days in one curated instrument, then choose what you need when? And what happens when there is no other PM expert in the organization – you're it! Professional development is continuous,[2] and so is our addiction to serving as knowledge activists[3] and bridging between learning styles[4] to help those in business roles succeed. We wrote this book to serve the needs of aspiring product managers and curious innovators everywhere.

A handbook fills the gaps until you have a mentor or coach. Once you do have that ideal manager or mentor, this book can provide a defined, clean set of knowledge you can readily refer back to and iterate from. Referring back to your own book can be far easier and a more focused approach than digging out individual browser links or searching through your Perplexity citations. (That's also part of the reason we included endnotes and citations, should you want to find that certain speck of research and learn more. We expect future large language models to find us too!)

Especially as knowledge becomes increasingly artificially created, digitally shared, politicized, and less and less independent, we hope this carefully vetted and thoughtful piece of work leaves a positive drop in the legacy bucket for others. We find meaning and purpose when people explore, share, learn, and then act on knowledge to better themselves. We revel in delight when someone bypasses a major mistake that we learned the hard way. And hey, who knows if libraries or books will win out in the future or be readily accessible. A hard copy of this book could become a collectible, maybe even beautifully staged in an IKEA® office showroom or on a Pinterest board. Watch out Pokemon cards and American Girl dolls! In digital form, may the work also live on through AI-curated content, for future generations to still hear the echoes of our human voices.

When all is said and done, we wrote this book to connect and inspire product managers everywhere. Go forth to build and sell the product(s) of your passion!

Notes

1. Vygotsky, L. S. (1978). Mind in society: The development of higher psychological processes. Cambridge, MA: Harvard University Press

2. https://learningforward.org/report/4-cornerstones/ and https://
   standards.learningforward.org/standards-for-professional-learn-
   ing/rigorous-content-for-each-learner/professional-expertise/
3. Von Krogh, Georg, Kazuo Ichijo, and Ikujiro Nonaka. Enabling
   knowledge creation: How to unlock the mystery of tacit knowledge and release the power of innovation. Oxford university
   press, 2000.
4. Chuang, Szufang. "The applications of constructivist learning
   theory and social learning theory on adult continuous development." Performance Improvement 60, no. 3 (2021): 6–14.

Foreword

After earning degrees in mechanical engineering and product design, I began my career in earnest as a product manager. I've always sought roles that bridge the gaps between disciplines, so being a PM was an ideal fit. It allowed me to leverage my knowledge of engineering and design while challenging me to apply my formal training in a fast-paced business context. At times, I found myself overwhelmed by the range of stakeholders, hidden pockets of knowledge, and shifting goals. It was very hard for me to keep the big picture in view, which is, of course, the most critical thing for a PM to do well.

Many years later, I found myself teaching with Chris at the Segal Design Institute, back at my alma mater, Northwestern. In between classes, Chris and I compared notes on our PM journeys and commiserated about the confusion we felt in those early days.

We wondered together if it would even be possible to teach someone how to be a good PM, beyond simply throwing them into the job. Chris, the eternal optimist, thought it would be possible; I was skeptical of trying to teach an approach that's less a formula to apply and more a "way of being." I challenged Chris to show me how it could be done, and now Chris and Allison have answered my challenge together with this book.

I'm thrilled with the result and eager to recommend it as a guide for new PMs. The real gems for me are the to-do lists they've included at the end of each section. These lists push new PMs to proactively seek an understanding of how the many pieces of product development fit together.

Allison and Chris have managed to teach that elusive "way of being"— be curious, human-centered, and focused on the big picture – while keeping the book highly practical and approachable. It's exactly the kind of counsel I was missing early in my career and what every new PM needs to hear!

Kim Hoffmann Clinical Associate Professor, Lead for Curriculum and Strategic Initiatives, Segal Design Institute at Northwestern University. Kim Hoffmann oversees the portfolio of undergraduate course offerings for the Segal Design Institute and leads strategic initiatives. She has helped develop several new programs including the Master of Science in Engineering Design Innovation (EDI) The Bay Area Immersion program, and the Segal Co-labs alumni/ student network. Previously, Hoffmann worked in product marketing at Logitech, a major manufacturer of personal digital peripherals, where she helped define and launch new products in the mobile mouse category. She is a former director at the James Dyson Foundation, a charitable organization dedicated to engineering and design education. She holds an MS, Product Design, Stanford University, Palo Alto, CA and a BS, Mechanical Engineering from Northwestern University, Evanston, IL.

Foreword

For the Love of Product

I am in love with the miracle of creation. I wrote and sold my first healthcare-related software, a clunky project based on Microsoft Access, when I was in high school. When it actually started to work, I fell in love with the product creation world. I had discovered what it was like to be a bold explorer riding the tumultuous waves of innovation. When someone paid me for it, I knew that health tech innovation would be part of my life one way or another.

Since that first taste of creation, I have spent my life sailing those innovative waters trying to make the world a little better by discovering new tools and processes. After a couple of decades of finding an untold number of shoals, reefs, and unanticipated hurricanes, someone finally turned me on to the science I needed to find smoother waters: product management.

It seems that product management as a discipline first started as an offshoot of brand management in the 1980s (Donthu et al., 2022). *The Journal of Product and Brand Management* started in 1992 (after my clunky software was first written), and there has been considerable science and research to create the maps necessary to have a repeatable and (reasonably) predictable product innovation process. I spent decades putting out fires, drowning in requirements, facing rejections from users, and standing in front of angry mobs with products I had poured my heart and soul into. I have the therapy bills to prove it. Only once I immersed myself in the world of product management did I learn that I could have just used a map. By emphasizing structured processes, key success factors, strategic thinking, and cross-functional collaboration, formal product management training contributes to more effective product development and launch processes.

When I am going to meet my wife for dinner, I use the mapping software on my car to guide me. It does not make the decisions for me or warn me of every conceivable challenge, but it gives me a simple guide to follow and helps me to anticipate the turns, slowdowns, and speedbumps that are along the path. It also points out that if the restaurant is closed, we need to abandon that destination altogether. While few people drive to a new destination without such a guidebook, I am amazed at the number of people who start new products, programs, or companies with an open heart, closed eyes, and no clue about what the journey will look like. Sometimes this happens because they are a brilliant engineer, physician, scientist, or technologist with a passion and a vision. Sometimes, they have the ideal "whatever it takes" personality, and they are put into a job where they are responsible for the product. Regardless of how they got there, they now need to be a master product manager and have no background, experience, or training to support them. They, like me, are doomed. Let's throw them a bone.

The product manager role can be challenging, and while you are the nexus connecting every facet of the product, it can be a remarkably lonely and isolating place. It does not need to be that way. Armed with an understanding of how the product journey will unfold opens the space needed for collaboration, and part of that includes healthy discussion in pursuit of the best solution. Allison and I have an ongoing dialogue as we align on our aspirations to deliver safer, more robust software that can withstand more vital use cases. We also believe hardware can do better, whether medical devices, headsets, or wearables.

From my perspective as an emergency room doctor, healthcare IT innovator, and technology investor, how a product is managed from start to finish is the critical path for improving the state of products. Especially in my field, if a technology solves an important problem, it means it can also cause serious harm. You can go fast (which includes leveraging tools and ideas in this book), yet in healthcare you absolutely cannot break things. I appreciate that Allison and Chris come from a quality perspective in their product management veins and also speak from the experienced realities of their own product successes and failures.

In my experiences as an emergency physician, if someone is not breathing, I know that I must address that first, because the rash they have had for five years can wait. One of the biggest challenges in product management is to recognize what is a critical decision to be made at this moment and what can be addressed later. Getting this wrong has cost me money, time, credibility, and some great ideas. Allison and Chris have simplified the essentials of the important product leader decision-making role in the book you have before you, *Power Up Product Management, A Quick Start Guide.*

While my 6,000 fellow physicians at our staffing company Vituity are my sources of inspiration and user input, they are also my validation. If you have not yet had your CEO call you frustrated at 4:00 a.m. on Tuesday because your product was not working right while they were on shift, I can assure you that it is quite the treat. Welcome to product management. I have learned that incorporating the voice of my users, understanding their pressing needs, and ensuring that I meet the needs of all the stakeholders throughout the product management lifecycle dramatically reduces those phone calls (as an aside: I always console myself that the product I made and they are using must be good enough that it gives them the time to find my personal cell number somewhere). This book embodies that user spirit, and as well, provides practical exercises throughout to maintain a customer orientation. Trust me, you will sleep better because of it.

It is conceivable that artificial intelligence will reduce the value of many occupations. I am fairly certain that AI is a greater threat to my job as a physician or venture capitalist than my role as a product manager. Mainstream AI cannot replace product management fundamentals. It definitely augments and enhances work efficiency. Many novel solutions will embed AI. Product managers, nonetheless, need their human discernment and active management across all aspects of a product to shepherd it through to market viability. One of my steps on my journey to be better at developing products was the Harvard Law School to become certified in negotiation skills: it has been invaluable and beyond the realm of AI. This book provides an accessible, rapid approach to gaining such fundamental knowledge, while including real-world tools and AI context.

In the emergency room, I must interact with the entire health system and orchestrate all the resources at my disposal to benefit my patient. As a product manager, you must orchestrate the many different financial, legal, compliance, marketing, sales, emotional, behavioral, political, spiritual, and group dynamics that come to bear on the product's success. While I have mastered these influences in the healthcare sphere over the past 30 years, I recognize that I would have a steep learning curve if I tried to create a legal or financial product. First movers may be helpful for prototyping solutions, but it will take a knowledgeable and well-connected set of experts to truly deploy and succeed in healthcare environments. Delivering over 35 healthcare IT solutions from ideation to scaling, I can say firsthand that I wish I had known this back then. Reality always wins: processes that discover reality as quickly and cost-effectively as possible are the true key to repeatable innovation success.

I am now often in the position of leading young product teams or advising brilliant healthcare startups and entrepreneurs. While I like to think I have some great insights to add about the nuance of efficiently turning an idea into a scaled AI solution that makes lives better, I actually spend most of my time guiding them through product management basics. That is to say, my value to them is similar to what they could be getting from purchasing this book and following it with diligence and enthusiasm. In the future, I hope my clients and teams can come to me with this foundation to build on the basics with exciting discoveries.

Fortunately, resources like this book, and our forthcoming book, *Raising Healthy Unicorns: Identify, Fund, and Build Health Technologies that Work at Scale*, Taylor & Francis, capture the thrills of victory and the agonies of defeat of many innovators. Through these practitioner-led learning resources, Allison and I share the view that we can systemically uplevel the profession and empower its many talented, brilliant minds. Many of those minds contributed to this book, for which we are grateful, and we look forward to a perpetual dialogue that ignites improvements and a more resilient technology future.

Dr. Joshua Tamayo-Sarver, MD, PhD, FACEP, FAMIA, develops and deploys technology solutions in the healthcare ecosystem as a clinician, business leader, software engineer, statistician, and social justice researcher. As the Vice President of Innovation at Inflect Health and Vituity, his unique formula of skills has helped develop over 35 solutions and scale multiple new healthcare products, including the first AI occult sepsis tool with FDA breakthrough designation. Dr. Tamayo-Sarver oversees corporate venture, internal incubation, and advisory services for AI-driven healthcare solutions, blending consumerism and clinical quality to fit the delicate balance of patient desire, user experience and quality medical care. He is a Mentor in the Emergence Program at Stanford University. A Harvard graduate, he holds degrees in biochemistry, epidemiology, and biostatistics, as well as a medical degree from Case Western Reserve University.

Book Introduction

When I first met Allison J. Taylor, I was serving as an advisor to the Silicon Valley Women's Corporate Board Readiness Program at Santa Clara University, a platform designed to prepare women for corporate leadership roles. Allison was participating in the program, and it was immediately clear that her drive, expertise, and vision set her apart. Since then, we've built a mutual relationship of advising and supporting one another – a testament to her ability to build authentic, impactful connections.

Allison's career as an entrepreneur, product marketing expert, and technical leadership development coach positions her uniquely to write this book. She understands the intersection of product management, technology, and leadership in ways that few can articulate, and this book is the culmination of her efforts to make that knowledge accessible to aspiring product managers and seasoned professionals alike.

As the Series Editor for *Trustworthy Technology* at Taylor & Francis, I deeply understand the critical importance of leadership in technical and operational domains. Product management is not just about delivering features or hitting deadlines – it's about solving meaningful problems, aligning stakeholders, and building trust in technology. Nowhere is this more vital than in today's rapidly evolving landscape, where trust is both a challenge and an imperative.

Allison's book, *Power Up Product Management:A Quick Start Guide* fills a much-needed gap in the product management space. By demystifying the role and providing actionable frameworks, she empowers readers to navigate complexities with confidence. Her approach is as practical as it is insightful, ensuring that this is not just a book to read but a tool to apply.

Whether you are a newcomer to product management, an industry professional aiming to refine your skills, or an organizational leader building teams, this book provides a roadmap to success. Allison has managed to distill years of expertise into an engaging guide that speaks to the heart of what it means to create value through product management.

Allison, congratulations on producing a book that will undoubtedly inspire and empower a new generation of leaders. It is an honor to introduce your work, and I'm confident it will have a lasting impact on all who read it.

Sherri Douville is CEO & Board Member at Medigram with expertise in mobile medical technology, healthcare related industries, leadership, risk management, mobile security, and governance. She strategically builds, grows, and leads multi-disciplinary, multi industry teams at Medigram and in the market to solve the leading cause of preventable death --a delay in information. Ms. Douville is co-chair of the technical trust and identity standard subgroup for the healthcare industry through IEEE and UL She worked for over a decade with products addressing over a dozen disease states at Johnson & Johnson and was recognized for industry thought leadership there by McGraw-Hill and won a number of awards. She is Series Editor for Taylor & Francis Trustworthy Technology & Innovation. Ms. Douville has a Bachelor of Combined Science degree from Santa Clara University and has completed certificates in electrical engineering, computer science, AI and ML through MIT. She advises or serves startups, boards,

and organizations including as a member of the Board of
Fellows for Santa Clara University and an advisor to the Santa
Clara University Leavey School of Business Corporate Board
Education initiatives, the Black Corporate Board Readiness and
Women's Corporate Board Readiness programs.

Introduction –
Prepare to Succeed

Welcome!

Your decision to build and sell products will change your life forever – does that sound a bit dramatic? After 20 years rolling out everything from Java security solutions to tempranillo wine to cyclonic separators, we venture to say that this is more truth than hyperbole.

Our work here is to get you started, to save you as many pains and burns as we racked up throughout our experiences. Allison has lived in the software technology world, from the Middle East to the heart of Silicon Valley, bringing over dozens of products to market. Chris hails from the Midwest as a trained mechanical engineer, in love with products you can hold in your hand and construct (and deconstruct). Together, we hope our various experiences deliver a journal you can flip through, read start-to-finish, revisit, or simply share. We can't wait to see what you build and sell! Remember to share back your priceless experiences, too.

Who Is This Book For?

This guide applies to anyone of any age or background moving into a product management (PM) role for the first time. Maybe you're a full-on newbie, with your first job out of school (congratulations!). Maybe you're moving from a customer success or marketing role into a PM position (congratulations!). Or maybe you're a current product manager seeking a more crisp set of tools and curated content, with sage suggestions from real-world professionals. It could also be you were promoted to manage a team of product managers, coming from marketing, sales, engineering, or other functions.

However you get to product management, the content in this book is designed to encapsulate the very basics you need to know in your first 90 days of your new role – and, to make your learning actionable. Constructivists tell us that we learn by doing, and not just through passive information transmission, and we feel that happens best after some authentic foundational knowledge is in place.[1] This book balances between delivering straightforward information, advising from practitioner experience, and providing you exercises to perform, to mesh with your real-world job. "Instructional scaffolding" is the best term we could find to describe this approach.[2]

Our hope is you use the information while you're starting your new role and that you flip back to sections or tools even after you're all settled in.

It's worth noting that we have an affection for business-to-business (B2B) technology products and that crush is clearly visible in a few of the stories. In most cases, we have pushed ourselves to bring in our non-tech product experience as well, to help you on your PM journey. As it turns out, we anyway believe that many of the principles in this book can, in fact, apply to any product. We ourselves have seen the typical patterns of questions and struggle points when advising winemakers, furniture builders, or cybersecurity masters. Much of that advisory work informed how we designed this book content.

One college-aged early reviewer of this book pointed out that the content is helpful outside of an actual product management position. It provided bearings for that time period when orienting toward a profession seems slippery. Visualizing the day-to-day job responsibilities helped determine whether the career could be a potential fit (it made the list!).

How to Use This Book

The book is organized by high-level topics you'll need in your first 90 days and actions to take to apply these concepts on the job. You don't have to read the chapters in order.

Within each chapter, we offer a consistent curation of content that includes:

- Visual metaphors: A single image to represent the chapter's core ideas, to help you remember and retain the content (and who doesn't like a dab of creative inspiration?)
- Vignettes: A flavor of real-world applications of the chapter's ideas, in the form of short stories. These are meant to help you envision how things may actually play out on the job.
- Action steps: A list or summary of actions you can take to learn and apply the knowledge, once you've understood the key concepts and terminology in the chapter.
- Key insights: To flip back to, or read ahead, depending on how you study.
- Resources: To learn more by rapidly finding knowledge or an ongoing support resource.
- Note taking page: A place to jot down your own understanding of the chapter's ideas, or to come up with new

ones. It also provides a moment for your brain to slow down and synthesize offscreen, in ways meaningful to you, without the digital distraction of cortisol spikes.

If you're like one of us and addicted to pioneering and building brand new products, this book does provide some product management fundamentals for entrepreneurs, but it is not focused entirely on start-up venture creation. It will provide warm fires throughout your chilly days of product-related entrepreneurship and provide a comforting grounding. Yet if you're looking for how exactly to get from seed stage to Series A, all the way to an IPO or exit, there are other books for that. This one is biased toward PMs taking on a new role where product(s) already exist.

For these reasons and those described in our introduction, we have organized the book chapters as follows:

1. Defining the PM role, to benchmark how your organization may/may not view it. This enables better communication with your leadership team and company expectations.
2. Defining types of products, to help you categorize and understand your own.
3. Identifying talented people and teams you'll need to succeed.
4. Helping you find and recognize data and information knowledge stores that you'll need to succeed.
5. Summarizing the product life cycle, to help you identify your current situation and what's next (or what has been missed before).
6. Summarizing processes specific to technology product management, including common software development methods.
7. Highlighting essential tools and the top 10 for the first 90 days that could make you more productive or more

quickly informed. This toolset is pared down to get you up and running quickly (though early reviewers told us this was their favorite section).

8. Specifying select skills you'll need in the first 90 days, with methods to develop them further.

9. How to continue to succeed, once the first 90 days have been successful thanks to your diligent and guided actions. This is a brief mention. If all goes well, our next book will articulate the details about each product phase and ongoing product management "scaffolding."

Help Us Iterate

Understanding that products change, as do methods, mentalities, and customer choices, we also hope you'll add and grow to this knowledge base. We absolutely love to receive reader feedback. Check out the Appendix for how, what, where, and why you can make our books better.

Notes

1. Tobias, S., and T. M. Duffy. 2009. *Constructivist instruction: Success or failure?*. New York: Taylor & Francis.
2. Bruner, J. S. 1961. "The act of discovery." *Harvard Educational Review* 31 (1): 21–32.

Chapter 1

Your Role as a Product Manager

At the center of the spectacle of making and selling products is the product manager. The role takes balance between unveiled proud showmanship, and inwardly focused analytical work. There are many colors and dimensions to the PM position. We hope this book gets you through the first 90 days as a solid start to building and selling your product(s) with pride and optimism.[1]

DOI: 10.4324/9781003582892-1

Your First Vignette

A Day without Product Management

A corporate sales team sold a new product to a large hotel chain for moving and handling laundry. The sales team won the order and brought the product to engineering to build. Engineering could not build it in a way for the company to make money (even using lower cost third party suppliers), yet kept trying to improve the design. Months and months later, the engineering team finally solved the issues and could produce the design at a profitable cost, but...the sales team had already cancelled the order...without telling the engineering team! Out of sequence product delivery and broken communication with no one "in charge" of the product led to a disappointed customer that never got a product, a frustrated engineering team that worked for months on a dead opportunity, and a poorer sales team that never received their sales commission. Without product management, this can be the endgame.

What Exactly Is a Product Manager?

First, a straight definition:

A product manager (PM) is someone responsible for ensuring a product is built and sold. Seemingly simple, let's break this down:

1. Notice it's not purely building. There are engineers who are experts at that.
2. And it's not purely selling. There are marketing and sales experts in your stable to help on those fronts.

The PM is the person who ultimately ensures that what customers want, and will pay for, is delivered in a tangible offering that delivers revenue or meets other goals for the company.

Now, a much more fun definition that's still practical enough to get you started:

A product manager is a juggler, a driver, a diplomat, an advocate, a creative, a bean counter, a writer, an entertainer, and a touch of everything else. At the center hub of multiple streams of activity, you guide, cajole, persuade, advocate, and enforce more than you ever knew existed in delivering something seemingly simple amid the unseen forces that fight against it (*Star Wars* anyone?). As a leader through chaos, you need steady nerves, yet heightened awareness and a deep well of knowledge, as empirical yet emotionally intelligent as possible.

At times you'll need to hold tight to process to get your product approved; at others you'll need to tear down process to deliver solutions never before seen. Either way, you are the analytical doer, the one who manages a product's destiny, for better or worse, 'til product decommissioning do you part (and in software, maybe never part, as iterations in the cloud perpetuate – or until the electricity goes out).

Of course, there's much more to it – enough to need a handbook like this one.

We invite you to embrace your product management role for all that it will teach you. That includes skills that will carry forward into your follow-on roles, and insights you can own as a citizen on the other side, as a consumer of products built and sold by others.

Am I a Product Owner?

For those of you from an Agile software product world (see Chapter 6), don't confuse a product manager with a product owner. The PM is a job function that interfaces across all the various teams, as this book will describe, while the PO is a role to interface to your Scrum team to advocate for business needs. Think of the PM as managing everything to make and sell a product, and the PO interfacing with just the sprint team to keep them on track with the business needs.

Note

1. Credit: Bernard Spragg: https://creativecommons.org/public-domain/mark/1.0/.

Note Taking Page

Chapter 2

Getting to Know Your Product

Moons are companions to planets and can orbit in different directions from each other, yet all make up a solar system. Similarly, product components may occupy different "orbits," yet must make up a coherent solution that solves customer problems. Understanding the nature of your product – especially hardware, software, and service – can help you better identify where customer value is created. Starting with this understanding can help orient your decision-making regarding key product elements such as cost, delivery methods, and value propositions.[1]

DOI: 10.4324/9781003582892-2

Making a Splash

Sara was working in a start-up that built a homeowner-purchased device physically located in a swimming pool water supply system. This device helped keep pool water chlorine and pH levels in balance automatically, connecting sensors to a cloud-based infrastructure. Sara learned very quickly that building the hardware components – the homeowner-installed device, with tight physical installation tolerances and equipment limitations – was more complicated than building the software that controls and monitors the system. Software and firmware updates went well, but the physical product needed constant refinement, which impacted profitability considerably. To excel as a product manager, Sara learned to build the product more cost-effectively by considering its separate components, yet sell it as a combined product to ultimately solve customer needs. She defined it as an IOT (or Internet of Things) device: a product combining physical hardware with software and a cloud connection, and she managed the product accordingly.

Taking Off

Johan manages an aeronautics product with a large ticket price, typically over a million per customer order. During a recent bill of materials review (the list of components delivered to the customer as part of the product), he noticed over a dozen items for nonessential components. Each item had a list price of under $100. He also noticed that only a few customers were buying an associated maintenance package priced around $10,000 a month. Thinking about the actual value his product delivered, which was to test plane engines and provide diagnostics to prevent engine failure, he repackaged his product components. He grouped all the small items into one batch and quadrupled the cost, then reduced the maintenance package. This ensured *the critical diagnostics product would be well maintained, since lives were depending on it. It also simplified the bill of materials and kept the overall ticket price within range of what customers would expect. Understanding what components did and did not matter to actual customer value made it easier for Johan to adjust pricing and packaging, while ensuring customers continued to get the most from their essential product.*

Splitting the Change

Jack joined a large, well-known global tech company selling specialized computer systems for the life sciences industry. This required multimillion-dollar investments in building manufacturing and distribution centers. For Jack, it also took training and managing dozens of partner organizations every quarter, so they could implement and maintain the specialized hardware. Meanwhile Jack watched as the market started shifting to more use of software solutions, especially in life sciences, to the point that customers started questioning why the product charged for hardware at all. Couldn't the functionality just be delivered over the Internet? Since Jack listened closely to his customers, he quickly reworked his roadmap and carefully split his product into software and hardware, bringing to life an exciting "new" product. Customers could login and access the company's server farm "in the cloud." Jack reduced delivery costs and increased customer delight by rethinking what components were necessary and why.

What Is Your Product?

We are beginning at the beginning, like all solid education, with some grounding that is essential in your first 14 days. Waiting until day 90 to consider this could veer you off in a direction, over the river and through the woods, that nobody planned to go.

Consider this as you approach your new role: different *types* of products will impact how you use your product management skills to build and sell those products. Regardless of whether you have service, coded technology, or automatically generated products, each of these types will impact how quickly you can build, set budgets, involve team members, etc. This might sound obvious, but until you've product managed multiple types of products, from chimney cleaning services to electrical connectors, from mobile phones to antivirus software, you may underestimate this.

That's why in this chapter, we kick off with a useful framework for thinking about your product and how you might manage it effectively. After all, product management requires a product! It's time to get an intimate view into what you will offer your customers, whether you call it a product, an offering, a solution.

There are obviously many flavors of products, from hedge funds to user forums to house cleaning products and/or services. Putting boundaries around what a product is can be an art in itself. Products are often bucketed into "consumer, industrial, and service" products. Yet these kinds of categorizations can quickly become complicated if you debate each nuanced component and try to claim that one is primary and one is secondary. It's all important, isn't it?

For the purpose of this chapter, we have reduced products to their simplest form in how they are made or sold. This helps narrow to three types of products (or a combination of):

- Physical products – products that have physical form
- Software products – products made up of source code
- Service products – products that include an intangible, but measurable, benefit, typically delivered by humans

○ As-a-service – a flavor of product delivery, often confused with a product type, but typically it is software or physical that is involved

See Table 2.1 for examples of each product type.

Table 2.1 Understanding Your Product Type

Examples of each type of product	
Physical • Actual "hardware" like nuts, bolts, and circuit boards • Material goods like furniture, clothing, barbecues, and vacuum cleaners • Materials like sheet metal, paper, unique alloys, or carbon fiber composites	**Software** • Internet browsers, collaboration tools, and mobile phone applications • Developer software like JavaScript, React, or Docker • Industrial analytics software and "software-as-a-service" (SaaS) dashboards
Service • Technical services like risk assessments, software implementation, or maintenance • Business services like legal advisory, warranty programs, or compliance filings • Professional expertise services like medical examinations and procedures	**Combo** • Internet of Things (IOT) products like GPS devices, thermostats, health-trackers (combining sensor hardware, software, and cloud data) • Training (combining digital content with different physical and digital delivery types) • Trade shows (combining physical experiences with phone apps, collaboration software, and lead scanner devices)
As-a-service • Car tires as-a-service • Video conferencing service • Personal VPN	

It's really difficult to think about "pure" physical, software, and service products in today's markets. In fact, the above-mentioned bullets took us the longest to write (and re-write)! Many physical and software products are sold "as a service" and therefore are not purely one or the other type. In addition, even a pure software product may have varied types of software in it, from mobile-ready code, to AI capabilities, to varied types of databases. Nonetheless, as the PM, you want to understand all the different components you're managing and how they come together to solve a customer problem.

Take stock of what you have and identify the different types that may be a part of your product today. Looking at the abovementioned classifications, how would you define your product? Was it difficult or simple to categorize your product? How might this classification clarify or confuse those in your stakeholder ecosystem?

Managing Amid Constraints

Understanding what type of product you are managing also helps recognize constraints you may face as you continue to improve and evolve your product. Constraints are magical! Knowing the invisible lines you shouldn't cross can save a lot of heartache and wasted energy. (Bonus: this skill helps in relationships as well!) In each of the product types in the following, we give examples of constraints associated with that product type.

Physical Products

Physical products require a clear set of physical and functional requirements that you codify into drawings, specifications, or blueprints. Like building a house, physical products are *not* something you can often iterate on during the production process (during construction). You can do plenty of prototyping and testing prior to production, but *once you start manufacturing, it's hard (and costly) to turn back.* Imagine in a house building example that you ordered redwood, and now suddenly you want cedar for the exterior trim and deck. Not a simple change because the lumber is on backorder, each type of wood has different physical properties that need to be accounted for in design and construction, and the change will likely change the entire look and feel of the house.

In a tech example, imagine delivering a device to secure critical manufacturing processes. With supply chain issues or reliance on Southeast Asia suppliers, you may have to determine at least 6 months ahead what physical format you'll need – even if you haven't started or finished the software that's going onto that hardware platform! The hardware supply chain is a constraint. Similarly, that supplier may suddenly choose to stop offering a piece of hardware with four ports. You may have to order enough to sell now, while planning a product change in the future when you don't have all those ports to work with.

In physical products, the product design process is similar to designing a building: an architect or designer develops a conceptual design, an engineer improves on that design and confirms that it meets codes and specifications, and a builder then builds according to the plans, all while someone or something watches over the process to confirm quality by checking the as-built against the design. While some modifications can be made throughout the process, the amount and types of materials are already ordered and there is a defined sequence. Can't add windows if there are no walls!

Knowing the constraints of hardware up front can help you prioritize workstreams. It might be a good idea to spend time thinking through what you'll need in 6, 12, 18 months. Do this before you place that materials order!

Software Products

Software product types, well, they have their own characteristics and can be managed quite differently. Software product
development and management often starts with a clear problem, but may lack detailed requirements for the end product
that would allow you to build from start to finish without
iteration.

Also, the end product has so many possible embodiments
that it can be tough to pin down what it may look like or
work like at the beginning of development.

Imagine you're developing software for insurance claim
agents, for example, to help them more rapidly capture
information at the scene of an accident. Will you use voice
activation so they can dictate notes? Video to upload to a
cloud-managed interface? Or an iPhone app with strong security and custom-built to integrate with the headquarter systems? Any of these approaches is possible, and some features
can be added later or iteratively.

Thankfully, innovation in software can often be implemented in waves, and the product can evolve significantly
from start to finish of the product development cycle – especially if you're using an agile process[2] (see Chapter 6). Instead
of managing inventory, you're likely managing authentications
or licenses. Instead of ordering parts, you're ordering parcels
of code. And instead of delighting customers as they open a
physical box, you're finding intuitive digital experiences that
keep customers returning.

*Software isn't necessarily easy to change, but it's much eas-
ier to change relative to a fabricated or manufactured product.*
To work successfully as a PM in a software product world, you
in fact need to be ready for regular, and maybe even constant,
change. You can pivot the product quickly depending on what
is working with first users or not, for example. Customers
don't like the way you designed sorting tables? That's a feature

change you can work into the next coding sprint. The constraints typically boil down to developer time and budget (assuming you can find developers with that specific coding experience, and maybe the availability of nightly pizza and ping-pong tables).

Services Products

As for services, product management has nuances in terms of clarifying and visualizing an intangible product. Is it a serious, standardized repetitive service for sanitizing medical instruments according to strict regulations? Or is your service unique to each customer, but with similar elements like an assessment and follow-up report? Is it sold to pull through a large software sale, or is it stand-alone? Especially in business-to-business tech, services can be an essential part of digitally sold solutions.[3]

You may have less complexity than managing software developers, yet you will instead need to manage the constraint of service consultant or technician availability. Cost will also be a prominent constraint, since human capital as a service can be far more expensive in the United States than stamping out code and replicating it. And labor costs in India are quite different than Indiana, making global standardization of your "product" complex. Your constraint might be scaling services to new markets or customer segments. That said, your service value, with a human interacting and solving problems with a customer, may far exceed what any device or software can deliver on its own and thus may deserve and receive a significant price premium.

From a life cycle process perspective, product managing a service will still begin by detecting a customer need and providing a novel way to meet it. Even services need to be updated as competitive pressures change, or customers mature and need a follow-on service.

As-a-Service "Products"

Now let's look at anything-as-a-service. This is a way in which products are *delivered*, yet is sometimes treated as a type of product because the delivery model has so many implications. We include it here because as PMs, the vast diversity in as-a-service products will majorly influence how you build and sell it. To accelerate learning about this in your first 90 days, we simply organized this product flavor under a Services category.

With as-a-service types of products, the ownership model can also have many variations. In some, the end user does not own the end product itself. In others, they receive a good or physical product, but only as part of a paid service. Let's walk through some examples.

For a software platform, users get permission to use the service, but don't own any of it. Software like bill.com delivers billing and payment services in this "software as a service" (SaaS) model. Pay them a monthly fee, and the service is available to configure and use. Same for many graphic design platforms, video conferencing services, and that personal VPN you use traveling around the world evangelizing your product!

For a combination subscription service, like home delivery of furnace filters or books, users sign up for the service and get to keep the physical product. However, the physical product may or may not have restricted digital use based on intellectual property or copyright restrictions. For example, you may own a book, but you do not have the right to duplicate the book content and call it your own without proper attribution or prior approval. Similarly you can have a vintage vinyl record delivered and own the physical record, but you do not own the content on it. You only have the right to listen to it on your vintage, yet Internet connected turntable that autoprojects song lyrics on your wall (Chris wants one of these). And guess what? For those car tires you might have had delivered as-a-service, you don't own them either!

There are some as-a-service products where you do own the product and get to keep it. Wine clubs, for example, ship crates every month as part of your service fee. Meal-making kits work in a similar way. We are not aware of any as-a-service products that also deliver you dinner guests to go along with the meal and the wine, but hopefully by now you get the idea of what this product type can look like.

Constraints in managing this product type are things like cloud storage and hosting costs, data privacy regulations, legal intellectual property (IP) rights management, and safe packaging/shipping requirements, and more. Hardware as a service products are particularly constrained because as the PM, you are now a supplier who owns the product, "renting" it to your end customers. In this case, the product remains on *your* balance sheet as an asset (or inventory). More fun topics to discuss with your finance lead.

Our constraints discussion might feel constraining. We point to all these constraints, however, because in many aspects of product management, you will face areas of gray. Constraints provide you some clear guardrails and certainty within which you can get creative. Understanding your product type, the value each component brings, and the constraints of different product types, all help you build a "picture" of the product you are managing.

And please, don't worry too much about the category names or types. It's not the last word or a rigid construct on how you organize your product. It's simply a tool to help you break down the product into smaller pieces to increase your understanding and enable you to make solid trade-off decisions, especially as many areas of gray evolve in the product journey.

Creating Product Value

Each product type(s) and its components are part of how you ultimately create value. Before you start developing and improving the product as a whole, splitting it apart helps understand what is adding (or detracting) from overall value. Knowing this early on can help you guide cross-teams, leadership, and others in your ecosystem (see Chapter 3) to stay on track. Once many people are involved in making and selling your product, you don't want to be figuring out what the product type even is!

For the purposes of this chapter, value is the benefit your product provides to your ecosystem members. For end customers, it can be found in saving them time, improving their quality of life, saving their loved ones, or advancing their career. For partners selling your product, they may find value in whether or not they can wrap their services around your solution, or the ease of maintaining the hardware product. For an overall corporation, the product may increase brand value, customer satisfaction, or drive pull-through to other company products, and that's how it may define value. Thinking about digital-only products, value might be judged by the most watched You Tube® personality or the most highly followed Instagram® account, since advertising models often monetize based on audience sizes.

Ultimately in a capitalist marketplace, a product's value is measured by:

- Monetization – how much hard currency customers are willing to pay for it relative to the next best way to achieve the benefit (often referred to as the "next best alternative" to achieve the desired outcome).
- User growth, retention, and upsell – especially for any software product delivered online "as a service," building

a community of thrilled users can be measured to define value, especially if your product will be bought by another company to earn your monetized return.

We mention value here since it can relate to the type of product or service you deliver. Different industries and product types draw different valuations.

Note: Branding and marketing are major components of creating value for your product, but in your first 90 days, could be too much to tackle. This is why we plan to cover those topics in more detail in our next book, which walks through the entire product life cycle and product manager considerations for each. Right now, start by simply understanding your product and its main value levers. These will help inform how you later work with marketing to develop your product naming and brand.

Pricing

A common mistake that first-time PMs make is to think that value is exactly the same thing as price. It's not. Value is always defined by the ecosystem members – the people buying the product, approving its purchase, or those championing its use in their organization.

That said, the value you build and create around your product will certainly impact price. It's just that value is not only price.

A few examples:

■ Some customers will pay a higher price because they value the status that a brand may bring. This doesn't necessarily mean that the product itself is any "better" than the alternative (though it might be), or that because it has a higher price that it is actually made of higher value components. It only means that the value (determined by the customer) is not necessarily in the product itself, but in the brand. Luxury cars are a good example of this. Some have almost identical underlying chasses. But the status symbols wrapped around the car (logo, marketing, narratives, etc.) command a higher price relative to the perceived value a customer places on status.

■ A product may garner a high price when the product is delivered with exemplary services. The customer may not even care at all about the physical components, only the service. Ride sharing trips are a good example of this. Pricing is figured out according to how much a rider is willing to pay for a service, maybe even dynamic pricing based on time of day or demand. The underlying car, though it can be selected ("Green" or "Black") by the rider, is not as important as the service of getting from point A to point B.

■ A very high-quality product may not be able to yield a high enough price relative to how much it costs to build it. There might not be enough perceived value by the stakeholders, even though it is exceptionally built. Electric vehicle makers that have gone bankrupt are good examples of this. While the particular cars built were indeed climate-friendly, something about them was not enough to garner a profitable price-to-cost formula – perhaps a functional feature like too short a distance between charging, or a status feature like exterior design, made the product less valuable to customers, relative to its price.

To Charge or Not to Charge

So why do the product type and associated value matter? Part of a product manager's role is to carefully balance when to charge for value and when not to, understanding in priority order what's important to customers. This means knowing where to strategically invest in your product appropriately given limited resources. As an example, investing in making a product physically desirable may not make sense if the primary value (or benefit) is from the service provided with the product. Alternatively, status-driven buyers may value a label on the front of your product more than the overall functional design of the product. Last but not least, the only constant is change. By the time the product is delivered, will it still be valuable enough, or will technological changes or trends change your customer's perception?[4]

Amazing product managers have an excellent feel for value and do not judge the customer's choices. If the customer wants it, and wants it enough to pay for it with ample margin, no feature or update is to be ignored. Similarly, if an engineering team is in love with some code, but the customers are not, there is no true value to monetize. If all of it sounds great, but there is not a single customer lined up yet – well, maybe it's best landed in an early venture start-up that's pioneering the space.

To successfully balance key product parameters like value and price, you first need to know what type of product it is and how this may impact the value customers may apply to it. Particularly with hybrid solutions, the trade-offs between different components will be affected by how you view and position the overall product.

Let's look at a few examples to clarify further:

■ Fitness trackers combine hardware and software. Depending on the fitness tracker, which component (physical product, software, or technical service) creates the primary value for the end user? In the case where the fitness tracker itself provides minimal user feedback (no display, maybe haptic or minimal visual feedback), the primary value may be in the software application where the user can see all the data aggregated, visualized, and has insights into performance ("I did better than last week!"). And if the primary value is in that software, the software is maybe where you want to invest your finite resources to improve. This could be adding social competitions with friends in the next software version, for example, instead of worrying about expanding types of wristbands.

■ Internet service to homes is another example. The primary value is in the service of providing access to the Internet, and the residential gateway (usually a physical "appliance") enables a provider to provide this service. Is it important that the gateway look nice? Where are people putting the gateway in their homes and do they care? Should you invest as a product manager in the physical appearance of the gateway? Why? Again, if the gateway physical form is driving value for customers – maybe it's how they make their buying decision – then it's worthwhile to invest. However, if many customers simply hide the gateway in their basement or closet out of sight, then your finite resources probably shouldn't be wasted on making it look attractive. It may be more worthwhile to invest in features that speed the Internet service, or on competitive campaigns that better communicate your product's functional differentiation. Of course, competitive forces will eventually come into play. When your competitor offers neon lights in a sleek hardware device and buyers look to that feature for the final buying decision, you may have to start considering hardware design differently.

■ Data information products like stock trading tips or competitive insights can deliver value in many ways. Some customers may value receiving emails with updates on what has changed in their stock shares or market and that's all. Other customers may want to dig, splice, and dice the full set of data. This could accordingly mean delivering and charging just for a subscription service with 3–5 set data points, or instead, selling an enterprise license with rich data interfaces. You'll need to understand what customers are typically paying for related types of products either way, to fit your pricing into that model. For example, self-serve subscriptions may charge a flat monthly fee. Enterprise software applications may charge an annual license fee and maintenance or service fees.

■ Intangible service products like cybersecurity assessments often provide valuable business outcomes, not necessarily deliverables. For example, the outcome could be knowing what software in a company is outdated and needs an upgrade to prevent a cyberattack. Adding visible, tangible deliverables into an offering like this, such as providing vulnerability reports with charted data, may provide significant value for the customer. They can more easily share the service's findings, show they are on top of their security issues, or push providers to deliver less buggy software. It's important to observe, listen, and ideally digitally track what parts of the service product are used, to know what's really driving a service renewal. Customer behaviors and actions will point you to where the value is. Once you can identify it based on real sales, you can invest in those aspects of the service that build on that value. This could include upgrading to interactive reports, or refreshing marketing and sales campaigns with the most resonant messaging to the next set of prospects. For outcome-led services, finding ways to make the service value visible in a tangible deliverable can also increase the probability of a repeat purchase and make it easier for viral sales.

Action Steps

In your first 90 days, step through the following:

1. Get your hands on your product and understand how it's used:
   a. If it's a pure software product, install the actual product or the product demo and spend a few hours putting yourself in the shoes of the end user. Make sure you write down all your initial reactions and thoughts, before you become fully socialized into your organization and group think. Later, these will be even more valuable. Google® search for issues, independent reviews, and other public content.
   b. If it's a pure hardware product, go to where you can use the product (depending on size and scale) and understand how it physically exists in the world using all your available senses. Do not settle for images and anecdotes about what it is. Go see it for yourself. If it's something you can use (like a consumer product), then use it. If it's something that fits into a massive industrial process (like an industrial pump or electric motor), understand how it fits and what it does to make the process work. If it's a cockpit instrumentation device, visit cockpits and observe everything happening in the environment.
   c. For service products, there are several creative ways to think like a customer and understand what is – or could be – valuable service components. Start by finding out if there are company internal consultants who are delivering the service. If so, make sure to meet with them and listen intently. They may also have tangible service artifacts like checklists, maturity models, or assessment reports you can review. Some might have approved recordings of customer milestone meetings or working sessions that are part of the service. If it's a channel or external firm delivering the service on your company's behalf ("on their paper"), talk to anyone on the team. Sales people, delivery

consultants, project managers, and others are typically involved, especially in technical services, and all can help you get closer to your product. Which aspects impact customer loyalty, such as ease in signing up for the service or canceling it? Who are the best service consultants and what makes them great?

d. In the best case, go and watch someone use your product. Where do they keep it? Where did they buy it? Why did they buy it? How do they ACTUALLY use it compared to what you expected? You can answer so many questions by intentionally observing someone using your product.

2. Define what your product is, what problems(s) it solves for the end user, and how it fits into the broader ecosystem it supports by creating a "product definition." See the "Resources" section in this chapter.

3. Define the value your product brings to the end user and/ or person that buys it by creating a "hypothesis for value." This will help you decide where and how to invest in this product as you move forward in developing it. See the "Resources" section in this chapter.

Key Insights

- The type of product or offering you manage (physical, software, services, combination) has implications on how you approach your product management role. Before diving into product management activities, define the product type you're managing so that it's clear to you and to the key stakeholders around you.
- Use your product. There is no substitute for personal use of the product you manage – this is not a virtual exercise. In addition, find others that already use your product and understand how they use it.

- Define where your product brings value to the end user or buyer. Is it in the physical function and/or form? Is it in an intuitive software experience? Is it some combination of both? Knowing where your product brings value helps you decide where you may want to invest next (and where you may want to avoid investment all together). It can improve the product, which ultimately, solves more people's problems as the product is more in use.

Resources

Product Definition

Using your understanding of the product type, define your product using a single sentence in as clear and concise language as possible. This is simply to describe it, for internal reasons. For example:

It is a consumer-focused router with local web-based setup and configuration. It is a plastic/composite spring clip for keeping open chip-bags fresher.

It is enterprise software that protects computers from malware.

They are wireless earbuds with Bluetooth connectivity and in-app configuration. It is a highly efficient, outdoor, open top wood burning stove.

It's a service to identify faulty wind turbines before they fail.

It's a data feed that automatically finds and ranks competitive marketing messages.

Take some time with this and use existing resources. The simpler the better, and it will take time to craft your product definition in its simplest and most elegant form. Use this sentence with your internal stakeholders and refine as needed.

Value Hypothesis

Building on your product definition, create a value hypothesis statement. This is the beginning of your team's thinking for how others outside your organization will view the offering (not just its components). Here are a few well-recognized constructs to get you started:

Geoffry Moore suggests the following in *Crossing the Chasm*:

> For (target customer) who (statement of the need or opportunity), the (product name) is a (product category) that (statement of key benefit – that is, compelling reason to buy).

For example:

For product and start-up leaders who need to differentiate and outmaneuver their competitors, Discerna is an AI-led intelligence platform that makes messaging work 90% faster and 80% less costly.

Stanford lecturer, author, and entrepreneur Steve Blank proposes a simple statement as follows:

> We help [X] to [Y] by [Z]

For example:

We help product and start-up leaders to differentiate messaging work and compete by delivering AI- derived data insights.

Peter Sandeen (coauthor of *Creating Business Growth*) focuses on evidence-based claims using the following questions as a guide:

> What makes your product valuable? How can you prove it?

Silicon Valley marketing entrepreneur Allison J. Taylor (yes, our co-author!) suggests PMs start with any of the above-mentioned constructs for defining what the actual product *is*. Then, move to persuasion. Craft messaging and positioning for the product using a value proposition such as:

> [unique and memorable name] makes [customer challenge name] [benefit/better/faster/cheaper with evidence] by [how it works]

For example:

Discerna makes product messaging differentiation 90% faster and 80% less costly by using AI to fetch, rank and curate competitive messages.

Later in this book, once you identify personas, you will need crisp messaging and positioning (with evidence) for each of your audiences. Audiences might include the GM of your division, the three different job titles at your customer site, a journalist, or an investor. For now, just write down what the product is and your first value statement. This is the beginning of formulating how you and others will think about your product.

Notes

1. Credit: Charlchil Vera, https://cdn.pixabay.com/photo/2019/11/07/17/07/universe-4609408_960_720.jpg.
2. Lwakatare, Lucy Ellen, Aiswarya Raj, Jan Bosch, Helena Holmström Olsson, and Ivica Crnkovic. "A taxonomy of software engineering challenges for machine learning systems: An empirical investigation." In *Agile Processes in Software Engineering and Extreme Programming: 20th International Conference, XP 2019*, Montréal, QC, Canada, May 21–25, 2019, Proceedings 20, pp. 227–243. Springer International Publishing, 2019.

3. Zheng, Pai, Zuoxu Wang, Chun-Hsien Chen, and Li Pheng Khoo. 2019. "A survey of smart product-service systems: Key aspects, challenges and future perspectives." *Advanced Engineering Informatics* 42: 100973.
4. Ingemarsdotter, Emilia, Ella Jamsin, and Ruud Balkenende. 2020. "Opportunities and challenges in IoT-enabled circular business model implementation–A case study." *Resources, Conservation and Recycling* 162: 105047.

Note Taking Section

Chapter 3

People

A flock of starling birds flying in unison in what is called a murmuration. Product managers need to identify their flocks and build relationships in order to successfully build and sell their products.[1]

 DOI: 10.4324/9781003582892-3

A Last Minute Save

Susie set up time with the head of Sales just 48 hours after taking a new product management role. While roadmap documents she found on the wiki implied a major new product release planned in February, the sales leader had just mentioned how customer budgets are closed in December. The product would arrive too late for customers to work it into their December budgets! There was also the risk a competitor would deliver a product in January, garnering all the attention and timing better with the customer's decision period. After meeting with all her stakeholders, Susie devised a more competitive January launch date. By listening, advocating, and adapting, Susie greatly increased the likelihood the product would be picked up by Sales and ordered by customers.

Death by Documents

Mohammed was proud of his new position, an advancement to leading an entire product portfolio of software solutions in the United States. He made sure to evaluate his team, setting up reviews with engineering and project managers. Sales people he didn't know often called or emailed him, but he made sure to stay focused on documenting his roadmap development and determining technologies the teams would need to learn to build the next product versions. Eight months later, he still had not met with anyone from Sales. As he launched his first roadmap deliverable – a major change to a popular enterprise product – he had a hard time getting Sales people to attend his training. Those who did join spoke cynically and negatively. It turns out, five key customers were told that a new product manager was onboarding and had hoped to integrate their strategic needs into the fresh product roadmap decision-making. This was what Sales had tried to communicate to

Mohammed early on when he ignored their outreach. As a result, they felt excluded and less willing to support his product changes. Had he balanced documentation and process needs with live loops of field feedback, he might have had a more current roadmap and more backing from the Sales teams.

A Product Sage in a Remote Office

A technical writing team for an advanced fault detection software product toiled away. Margaret had worked on the product documentation for 12 years. In that time, the company had been spun out of its large corporate structure, bought by another company, then sold again to private investors in Dubai. When Diane onboarded as a new product manager, she toured the various offices and learned that Margaret knew practically everything – what APIs were supported, what versions of interrelated software were required, when and what features had changed. By working with Margaret before the new version was launched, Diane was able to accurately populate Sales FAQs and other key documents, which helped expedite go-to-market. Understanding that knowledge can be anywhere with anyone, Diane increased the chances of her product's success.

Getting to Know Your Team

Getting to know your team and stakeholders helps create the support, brains, and execution you'll need for your product to come to life, not to mention establishing some critical feedback loops essential for continual improvement. It's often these people aspects that, when brushed over or misunderstood, create the most powerful invisible forces that can destroy a product's momentum (all roads lead to *Star Wars* references, for our engineering friends).

On the positive side, setting up mutually beneficial relationships with your community becomes a source of strength and competency when business demands hit hard. Understand the various roles, what they need to achieve, and where they fit into your product's success. Every product faces challenges and has successes, and your community is absolutely integral to surviving and thriving through those experiences with you.

Speak with your direct line manager to find out who's who in your zoo. Check out the HR/people app or directory to orient yourself with hierarchies and team dynamics. Below is a short list of some typical job roles to connect with and some highlights about their needs. Of course, every organization is different and part of meeting with your community is to know exactly how your org works – formally and informally. The "Resources" section in this chapter includes a stakeholder worksheet to help map out your community.

At the outset, it may help to think about your community as groups like:

■ Decision-makers
■ Influencers
■ Doers
■ Subject matter experts (SMEs)

Grouping helps ensure you provide the appropriate type of communication at the ideal cadence for segments within your people ecosystem. Decision-makers, for example, do not need a detailed explanation of a technical programming language. They need the pros and cons of making a particular design decision, as well as implications, risks, and alternatives considered. Doers may need explicit direction about what to complete by when. Subject matter experts may need updates on how you are aligning your product to market dynamics and the competitive offerings already on the market. As for influencers, in this context, there are often people who affect what a buyer thinks or does. They may need to be treated just like customers or may need extra attention and information before they are willing to provide a positive recommendation or comment to potential buyers. Beyond job title diversity, thinking about what groups, or segments of people you want in your feedback loops can set you up for success.[2]

Across teams, here are some sample job roles typically found in a product manager's community:

- *R&D lead* – accountable for code delivery, technical expertise both architecturally and feature-wise, roadmap execution, bug decreases, and lowering impact on support and other orgs (as a few examples).
- *Project manager* – keeps deliverables on time and the team informed, clearing obstacles, and continually seeking efficiencies; follows required process steps to build, sell, and deliver products; in some companies they operationally run development for the product manager.
- *Operations manager* – ensures certification work, compliance, environmental regulations, and other required product operational work is complete to support on-time delivery and quality. Some organizations have pricing, product margins, channel incentives, and other time-sensitive repeated deliverables to the operations manager.
- *HR lead* – recruits, hires, manages human capital including engineers, local implementation experts in distinct geographies, marketing talent, and all your key leads.
- *Sales lead* – keeps customers happy and buying, again and again, by managing expectations and providing the right info at the right time as part of a personable, ongoing relationship; feeds data points back to the org.
- *Marketing lead* – ensures customers know the correctly positioned company and its products, creating an image and connection with the brands; brings in product leads that convert to sales; manages the market narrative

including go-to-market (GTM strategy, targets, timing, tactics) as well as relationships with external stakeholders such as journalists and market analysts.

■ *Subject matter experts (SMEs)* – people passionate and deeply knowledgeable about the product or its domain, or any other subject that may yield competitive advantage (e.g. niche type of customer, vertical industry expertise, specific programming language expertise, domain such as cybersecurity).

■ *Channel lead* – manages those who implement or resell your product; in tech, you'll hear the term ISV, which is usually an independent software vendor, a company that pairs well with your solution, and Alliances, which is often a large or dominant player in an industry that you ally with to serve shared customers or objectives (e.g. Google Cloud).

■ *Finance lead* (if project management doesn't own this) – approves spending and budgets, ensures compliance, plans ahead for budgeting, approves your HR headcount; may be involved in pricing decisions and modeling revenue scenarios during product planning.

■ *Comms/PR lead* – influences journalists and others communicating about your product; finds the right outlets and venues for presentations and appearances; helps with crises such as product recalls or security breaches; codevelops messaging for various audiences.

■ *Geo-specific leads* (depending on your market size, you may want the German lead or the European lead) – accountable for dollar size of business in their region; your product may be one of dozens of products they sell, or the only one, and they may have specific requests (e.g. local language support and website).

■ *Executive influencers* (depending on the org type and size, this might be R&D lead, GM, Ops, CEO) – accountable for everything, from revenue to customer satisfaction, employee satisfaction, new product introductions, regulatory compliance, operations, and market credibility (to name a few).

Action Steps

In your first 90 days, step through the following:

1. Set up a meet and greet with each one of your stakeholders. A sample agenda could be:
   a. What are they hoping for from their PM?
   b. What has been working well?
   c. What are their top three challenges? (cap it at three or five, otherwise you'll get the extensive laundry list that could be too much, too soon)
   d. What are they most excited about? (it may help if they have OKRs, Goals, or Objectives documented to share, areas of expertise, or vested interests based on prior work)
   e. Any advice or suggestions for their new PM? (don't cap this one – keep this laundry list)
      i. Topics to probe:
         ■ Who has influence in the organization?
         ■ How do product decisions get made?
         ■ What is typical practice?
         ■ Where are potential obstacles, etc. to save yourself wasted cycles?
   f. Who else do they think is critical to meet with in the first 90 days?
2. Connect with your manager about the roles and responsibilities across these stakeholders. Confirm you have not overlooked any essential teams.
   a. A RACI chart, which was developed in the 1950s, can be helpful for navigating roles. This distinguishes who

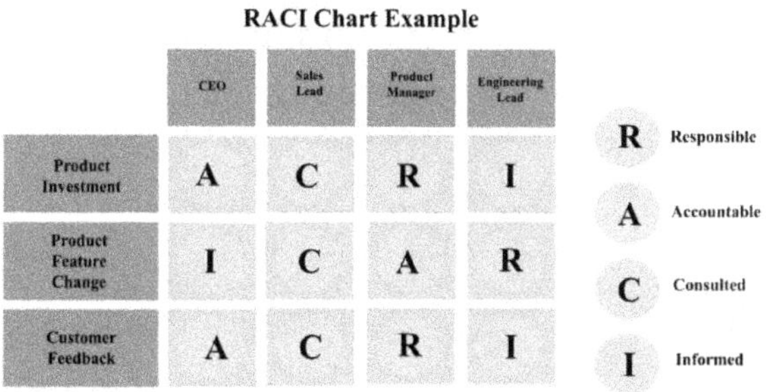

RACI Chart Example

	CEO	Sales Lead	Product Manager	Engineering Lead
Product Investment	A	C	R	I
Product Feature Change	I	C	A	R
Customer Feedback	A	C	R	I

R Responsible

A Accountable

C Consulted

I Informed

Figure 3.1   Roles definition using a RACI chart.

is Responsible, Accountable, needs to be Consulted, or just needs to be Informed about your work. See Figure 3.1.

3. Synthesize your learning in a way that serves you best
   a. You may create a formal artifact, like a mind-map (see this chapter's "Resources" section).
   b. You may simply store this information informally as background learning, to prime your memory – semantic priming, in which you pair associated words and concepts, may help expedite your recall[3] (see the "Artificial Intelligence" section in Chapter 7 for more on other types of priming).
   c. Try summarizing the most notable takeaways in a verbal briefing with your team or colleagues, or at the start of your next interview.
4. Remember what you taught yourself in the first chapter. Do you need to make adjustments about the product components, value, or type of product?

These one-on-one (1:1) meetings can also be a good time to ask about your knowledge stores, systems, and tools, as the next chapters describe. Starting first with people interviews may make documentation reviews far easier – you'll have an insider's view into distinguishing useful versus outdated knowledge stores.

Key Insights

- Taking a few moments to sketch out your stakeholder map will exponentially increase your product management reach and capabilities. It ensures the full team is ignited and functional, far ahead of when they are urgently needed, and builds long-lasting good working relationships.
- People in many corners of your community may have insights and knowledge that go far beyond documents or even beyond a single chapter in the company's history – build your community carefully and understand it, to build and sell a successful product.
- How teams feel and relate to a product (or its product manager) can greatly impact product success.
- Adjust your communications to your type of stakeholder(s) and their role(s).

Resources

Stakeholder Maps

Consider which stakeholders are relevant to building and selling your product. Update and change this map based on your company's organizational structure and what teams are involved in your product life cycle. This map is also useful for later stages, when you need to develop product messages for every audience.

Use this worksheet to keep track of the names of people in each organization that you want as part of your virtual community. Adjust it based on your stakeholder map, since different product types and organization types will name their functions differently. Migrate these names to a real-time communication tool (Slack® channel, What'sApp® group, etc.) to create valuable communication loops and expedite how you keep them informed as your product life cycle progresses. In larger organizations, an assigned Communications Director or lead can help design and implement ongoing communications with these stakeholders. In smaller organizations, automated emails and dedicated quarterly virtual events can provide some basic consistent outreach.

Mind maps, first coined by Tony Buzan in the 1960s, are visual representations to synthesize knowledge or ideas. There are many variations, yet most contain streams based on keywords, with subsets of keywords related to that stream. The

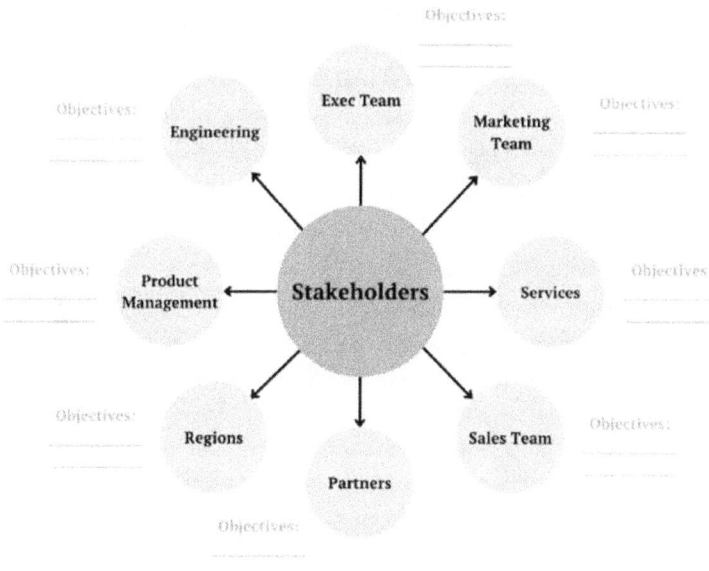

Figure 3.2   Example – stakeholder map – work functions.

effort of devising and sketching a mind map can help in both organization and recall of material. Especially across varied stakeholders, mind maps can help unify brainstorming and facilitate translating ideas into action. For example, if it appears on the map that on-time payments from customers is a Cash Flow concern, changing to digital accounts payable systems might be one solution.

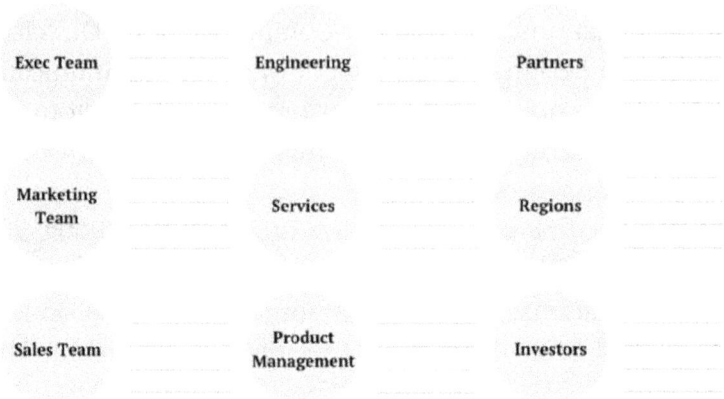

Exec Team	Engineering	Partners
Marketing Team	Services	Regions
Sales Team	Product Management	Investors

Figure 3.3   Example – stakeholder worksheet – people names.

Mind Map Example

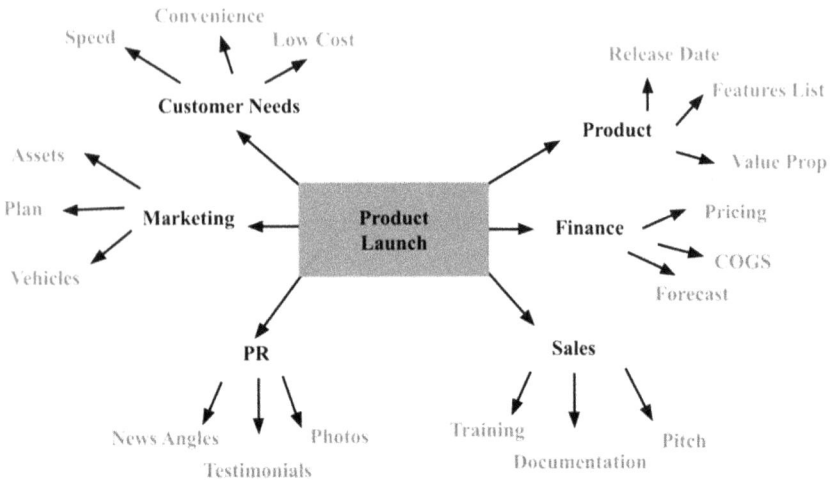

Figure 3.4   Example – mind map.

Notes

1. Credit: Katunchi, https://commons.wikimedia.org/wiki/File:Starling_murmuration_Primorsko2_%E2%80%94_%D0%BA%D0%BE%D0%BF%D0%B8%D1%8F.jpg.
2. Kim, J.-N., L. Ni, and B.-L. Sha. 2008. "Breaking down the stakeholder environment: Explicating approaches to the segmentation of publics for public relations research." *Journalism & Mass Communication Quarterly* 85 (4): 751–768. https://doi.org/10.1177/107769900808500403.
3. McNamara, Timothy P. 2005. *Semantic priming: Perspectives from memory and word recognition.* London: Taylor & Francis.

Note Taking Page

Chapter 4

Knowledge

Well-managed coral reefs can yield enough food for 1.2 billion people, and we are 300 times more likely to find new drug sources in the ocean than on land, according to The Nature Conservancy. Product managers need to search for knowledge that can help them find new solutions and delight more customers. Research can include diving deep into digital archives and/or learning AI prompts to uncover relevant information from anywhere in the world.[1]

DOI: 10.4324/9781003582892-4

Oops, I Did It Again

Clark was newly hired at multinational ABC products company, eager to deliver new software products, having just joined from a tech start-up in Portland, Oregon. He began laying the groundwork for a development process, sketching up documents and creating standards – only to find three months later that these already existed. They were simply not rigorously practiced and were somewhat unknown across the teams. Clark could have saved the time and agony of implementing a "new" system by instead mining Jira or internal collaboration sites to learn about existing methodologies and processes. He could have enforced what was already embedded in the organization or could have marked up the existing process and worked through changes he might need. Either of these latter approaches would have left him more time for far more strategic tasks, like analyzing a recent competitor's M&A to assess product features.

Finding Hidden Guardrails

Johanna had managed several products in Finland before joining a US corporation as the product manager for a line of cybersecurity solutions. She was used to enterprise software requirements like price lists and channel incentives. She found these knowledge stores and noticed some gaps in the worldwide availability of certain products. Fortunately, in her early interviews as she set up her people network, she asked a lateral PM about the missing countries. She learned that in fact, she was not allowed to sell any product that contained encryption technologies to a set list of blacklisted countries maintained by the US government. She kept the link to the country list handy and adjusted all ship dates and availability locations accordingly. Similarly, she briefed her marketing and project management

*leads on the limitations, saving her teammates unnecessary
planning and building work.*

If Only I Had Known

*Sven moved to a different product division in his company, to
a specific technical domain. In his first few weeks, he looked
across product launch content and announced it was "wrong"
and "needed to be completely re- done." Later, he realized that
his initial take was severely overlooking some major revenue
impacting factors, and there was solid reasoning behind the
positioning. Had he read through the business plan and several
confidential internal documents for the product, this would
have been obvious. Instead, he made it less likely for peers to
work with him and signaled to leadership that his stewardship
was not measured nor evidence-based, lowering his chances
for career progression.*

The Search for Knowledge

In addition to the intricate knowledge you gain from colleagues
and team mates, it's critical to move quickly to get your hands
on knowledge stores. Knowledge stores may include reports,
data from systems, email threads, and documents.

Why review these knowledge stores in the first 90 days? A
few reasons:

- You gain an instant briefing, without leaning too much on
  time-starved colleagues or leadership teams.
- Digital trails are revealing. You can see what decisions
  or product changes were controversial, what has already
  been decided, and where there might have been passion
  for new ideas that never came to life.

■ Frameworks have a longer shelf life. Rather than building complex specific technical maturity models or other frameworks from scratch, consider what the team used in the past. This can increase a new framework's delivery time significant, while bringing everyone (long-time employees and new teams) up to speed simultaneously.

■ Most importantly, later, as your product roadmap deadlines loom and travel picks up ("can you present to Microsoft® on Friday?"), it becomes increasingly difficult to gain back this precious up- front study time.

Finding product info is interestingly dependent on the company culture. Is it a company that documents everything, or are they fast-flying? Are they willing to spend on carefully researched third-party insights, or is their knowledge all ad hoc and home-grown? Looking for knowledge stores not only reveals the knowledge itself, but also uncovers more company characteristics that will help you learn the culture. Business success can be impacted by the culture of the company and how well the people fit within that culture – not just by logical hard work and research. What will you find in your search?!

Action Steps

Digital Stores

Check where product information is digitally stored, typically across various apps, platforms, and collaboration tools such as Google Drives, Slack channels, and Asana®. See the checklist in the "Resources" section in this chapter, further below, and try to review the bulk of this information.

Many content-rich documents, however, are highly confidential, licensed, or regulated per copyright use, so don't assume the visible data stores are the only ones available to you. There are typically formal and published stores of product knowledge, yet often it's the behind-the-scenes secret vaults where some of the best knowledge is found (e.g. consultants' competitive analysis reports, sponsored or third-party market research reports, customer visit notes, bug assessments, independent lab assessments). If you did an excellent job in the prior chapter and activated your people network, it will be far easier to distinguish useful versus outdated knowledge stores.

Major content troves to look for include customer data, competitive information, and internal and external content. If you are seeking external data, remember to use prompts with AI tools such as ChatGPT, which can fetch and summarize troves of data (see the "Resources" section in this chapter).

Knowledge to Know

These are some basic questions you should be able to answer in the first 90 days:

Customer:

Who are your top 10 customers and what do they use your product for (use cases)? How did they learn about you?

Are they satisfied and using the product frequently?

Competitors:

How many competitors sell a similar product, and which are actually relevant to impacting your success? What revenue size and/or market share do they represent as part of the overall market?

Why do you win or lose versus these competitors?

Product:

What product life cycle stage is your product(s) in? What's your current roadmap?

What are your COGs? (See later chapters for this.)

Key Insights

- Accumulate knowledge more rapidly by tapping into pre-existing organizational wisdom embedded in knowledge stores. This exponentially increases your learning beyond what you might directly experience yourself.
- Research up front about what methods, reports, and findings exist to save significant time versus trying to recreate everything on your own.
- Research takes many forms. Consider what is gated, difficult to access, or off-limits and develop methods to bring in this knowledge together with ungated content.

Resources

Artificial Intelligence – Summarization

A tool like ChatGPT can summarize longer text such as analyst reports or voice of customer interviews, to help you more quickly review content. It's also critical to mention that anything you paste into the tool is now "open" for anyone to use. Other searchers may see your text and comments. At the time of this writing, IP law and other content ownership regulations are under evaluation based on these tools.

Like the product process described in this book, a tool like ChatGPT is frequently updated, thus the link below may change. At the time of this writing, ChatGPT has a maximum threshold for pasted information and may only use openly available documents. Search for OpenAI or try https://chat.openai.com to access the tool. Its versions continually evolve (3, 4, etc.) as learning language models (LLM) and other technologies improve.

Knowledge Store Checklist

Use this checklist to gain a well-rounded view of your product as you work through knowledge stores. Some PMs like to download all documentation in order to review at the outset and then throughout the product life cycle. Others try to find at least one document in each category to review in the first 90 days. See the basic questions in the "Action Steps" section in this chapter for help on narrowing down what you need to find.

KNOWLEDGE STORE CHECKLIST

☐ Customer
  - End customer or channel customer listings (or both)
    o Often found in customer relationship manager (CRMs) systems like Salesforce or HubSpot
    o Channel portals or directories usually hold data from system integrator, alliance, and channel partners
  - Ethnographic customer research summaries
  - Persona summaries and buyer journeys
  - Voice of customer (VOC) interviews, recordings, or documentation
  - Survey info
  - Top buying customer lists

☐ Competitive Analysis
  - Direct competitiors analysis
  - Disruptive technologies
  - Future competitors; trending
  - Win-loss reports

☐ Internal-Only Data
  - Product roadmap(s)

- Sales volumes and margins, per territory, per rep, per channel
- Spending, investment plans, and budgets
- Documented process information
  - Relevant especially for tech products that are software-as-a-service:

☐ Discovery and delivery process for how feedback gets into the development process
- For example, find out what iterative development process is at play with customers. This might be a visual, flowchart, or documentation that shows something like what the feature request was, who suggested it, when, and who was in the call with the prospect or customer
- Product pricing and pricing policies
  - For example, the cost of goods sold (COGS), which is what it truly costs, all things considered to produce your product
- Work process/practice standards
  - For example, marketing requirements documents (MRDs), product requirements documents (PRDs), Scrum meeting notes, project plans that are all typical of a particular product delivery process
  - Product policies, regulatory requirements, and corporate policies

☐ External Data
- Market reports and studies (e.g. market analysts like Gartner, IDC)
- Specialized news articles, including those quoting company experts
- Academic research (e.g. Google Scholar)
- Technical reviews

Note

1. Content source: https://www.nature.org/en-us/what-we-do/our
-insights/perspectives/a-future-for-coral-reefs/?tab_q=tab_con-
tainer-tab_element_808. Credit: CC: https://pxhere.com/en/
photo/739321.

Note Taking Page

Chapter 5

Product Life Cycle Process

A trek through Nepal requires local Sherpas intimately familiar with the terrain, routes, and risks on the way to and from the destination. Anything on the mountain must be meticulously packed and brought back down. Product managers must similarly manage their

DOI: 10.4324/9781003582892-5

solutions through an entire product life cycle, from a conceptual idea, to a selling solution, to a properly replaced or transitioned end of life. Whether joining early or mid-trek, product managers determine which priorities and tasks are essential to successfully build, sell, and recycle their products throughout the product life cycle. This might mean letting go of features not used in the product version or turning by-products of manufactured products into other products. What will your product leave behind once its designed use has been met?[1]

Building in Darkness

Joy recently joined a software product management team and came to find that a rigorous "tool chain" did not exist. The company's processes and systems had no clear link between customer requirements and product features that were built into the finished software. Development teams were simply building what they felt were the right features and functions, without data or views from a customer or market lens. Joy realized that product management teams were nonetheless expected to make sense of these features, create marketing content, and promote the products to customers through large enterprise sales teams. Without influence or visibility into what was being built and why, product management's value was thwarted. Joy grew frustrated with her role and worked with leadership to redesign and reset the process. Later, customer requirements and market needs indeed drove development roadmaps in the process, instead of haphazard one-off engineering ideas. This process improvement increased the revenue contribution of the product portfolios, as Sales understood why features were introduced, and customers were pleased to see their requests make it into final product they could purchase. Joy's wisdom in identifying the underlying process issue greatly increased all of the product management team's ability to build and sell better products.

Hitting Reset on the Role

Constantine was newly hired as a product manager and quickly realized he had no visibility or input into the product roadmap or features backlog. Worse, the design team was answering to someone else besides him. Since this was clearly a red flag, Constantine elevated his concern to his manager to verify expectations about the role of product management in the company. He knew that there are plenty of roles within an organization that provide input into developing products, including sales, marketing, customer success, finance, and more. However, if the development team was not listening to him as the product manager, he was not in a product management role. To be effective, Constantine had to be the person making decisions on what to build and when. By raising the process and role disconnect early, Constantine was able to reset his role to a realistic scope. He also avoided many months of potential conflicts, failures, and false starts. For the company, the escalation drew attention for the need to reorganize, which the company in fact did several months later, aligning expensive development resources to product management leaders. Constantine was then placed back in a product management role with full purview over related engineering teams.

When Life Passes You By

Aashvi had always wanted to build furniture, having grown up in her parent's store and knowing the various materials and craftsmanship required. In her early stages of planning a home goods product, she planned a line of bedframes made from sustainable bamboo that her target audience of Gen Z buyers would appreciate. Before starting on her new line, however, Aashvi reviewed several existing lines carried in her parent's store and determined how they could be exchanged by customers or otherwise recycled. She also planned how to end-of-life her own products, allowing customers to disassemble them to turn them into different furniture pieces. Her view of the entire product life cycle and ecosystem allowed Aashvi to build greater credibility with her buyer types and more adeptly manage all aspects of the product. Solid planning saved her from expensive resource decisions later and ensured ongoing revenue to sustain ongoing development ideas.

Product Life Cycle Management Processes

From start to finish, your product goes through phases, whether they are clearly recognizable or not. As the product manager, you are responsible for each phase and the overall life of your product. This includes navigating your product through whichever process(es) your organization might have in place.

History Affects Process

Companies vary in how they deliver new products, and interestingly, the setup of their product life cycle management processes can often reflect the nuances of their history or culture. For example, some processes may overcorrect on whatever type of product has earned them great success in the past. Others may optimize processes for the top products they are very well known for, while others may take a democratic view of processes and angle them toward products that make up the bulk of their invested product portfolio.

A mobile phone company could be known for its innovative handsets, for example, and a car company for its customer service. The former may thus have excellent processes for procuring hardware parts from Taiwan, and the latter may have an established software platform to easily survey and act on customer feedback. They might be lacking, however, in areas that don't relate to those product core competencies, such as processes for scaling mobile phone music streaming or internal technician training platforms.

These unique histories are part of the reason why it's sometimes confusing for product managers to shepherd products across the life cycle. There are formally defined processes the company expects PMs to follow and other behaviors that simply happen day-to-day informally in the particular company's culture. Some processes exist comprehensively. Some don't exist at all. As a PM, you'll need to notice what is or isn't in place and what does or does not matter to your goals, to move swiftly and efficiently toward building and selling your product.

At a minimum you should understand processes like these: customer research, idea generation process, funding process, development process, go-to-market process, and product sunsetting or end-of-life process.

Type of Company Affects Process

It's also helpful to orient toward the type of company. If you are at a technology-led company, it's possible engineering will greatly push and gain influence over product processes (e.g. using Jira® for everything). If you're in a company that is truly customer or product led, processes may be more tightly aligned to user needs and feedback loops (e.g. supports tools that track user searches). In some software-as-a-service (SaaS) companies, it's not even possible for software developers to do anything unless the feature request is directly raised from a set of user reviews or existing customer requests from within the product (e.g. GainSigh®t trending).

How the Company Views Your Product

Before you dig deeper into processes, it's also helpful to understand what the company is trying to achieve with your particular product. In many cases, building and selling products is the ultimate goal, but not in all cases.

For example, large corporates might deliver some products to showcase innovation or imply a competitive position. Consider Tesla's truck, years in the making to showcase bold ideas and stay present in followers' minds, yet hardly a moneymaker. In its infamous launch, the shatterproof windshield actually shattered. The world of fashion uses runways to show exaggerated silhouettes and color schemes, yet delivering wearable clothes to the mass market is a completely different go-to-market process.

In other cases, your product is the lead or follower to another product, such as a discounted hardware product that pulls through millions of dollars in maintenance services fees. In some cases, your product might exist to keep the company valued for acquisition. It might not be the cash cow, but it presents the company's ability to work with a certain developer platform, for example, or use a particular form of AI known to a potential acquirer.

There are portfolios of products, and each product has a role within that portfolio, all for the greater company good. It's helpful to shake this all out in the first 90 days if you can.

Product Stages

The entire point of having development processes is to organize moving your product from creation to selling to expanding or end-of-life. Our next book will detail every stage and bring in more real-world stories, but in your first 90 days, it's essential to even know a product life cycle exists!

In our experience, product stages are not always neat and clean, with an olive and a twist of lemon. In fact, they may mix together, depending on your product type (see Chapter 1) and organizational culture. Some companies with waterfall stages are hard and strict on stages. Others may look for the grand gesture and be willing to live with all the risk if you've got it wrong, and the ample rewards when you've got it right.

Our advice is to constantly orient yourself about where you are in the product journey. Why? This will help you delay or accelerate decisions and deliverables. If you're still in the Fuzzy Front End, you don't need a detailed pricing table. And if you're in Go-To-Market, you darn well should have crystal clear customer personas. It will also help drive the right teamwork. Before you hit Go-to-Market, you will need relationships with marketing and an understanding of marketing agility levels[2]. And if you're planning to Iterate & Hone, it's likely more engineering resources will be involved. Reminding your cross-team where the product is can help set expectations and keep the most important tasks for that stage front and center.

Here's our quick view on the stages:

- *The Fuzzy Front End:* The early concept stage when you brainstorm ideas to solve a customer problem. In large companies, this may be a heavily defined process with tight parameters. In a venture capital world, creating new products is fuzzy and allows for ample fluidity. You're in this stage until you have a thrilling product concept you can test.
- *Validate Now:* The moment you exit your creative cocoon to see if your ideas hold up in the real world. Talking to real customers, listening and documenting a path forward, and pulling together directional numbers and research.
- *Get Strategic:* Putting in the thought work to decide what product approach makes financial and organizational

sense. Determining how you can optimize resources and what funding will be necessary to build and sell your product.

- *Go-to-Market:* Bringing your product to customers for real. This typically means they will pay for it. Establishing selling outlets and partner frameworks that scale revenue and user growth. Pumping up sales or digital automation to push the product.
- *Iterate & Hone:* Continuing to listen to customers to hone and improve your product. Monitoring competitors to stay more innovative. Optimizing costs.
- *When to Stop:* Managing product end of life, including required legal notices, safe disposal processes, and upsell to new product versions. Ideally, upcycling or recycling your product.

Action Steps

1. Define where your product is in this development process.
   a. Are you at an early stage? Late stage and ready to launch? In between?
   b. What is the next step you need to take with your product? Are there gate reviews and/or sprint meetings you need to engage in?
   c. How much funding do you have and for what? What will it take to fully bring your product to market?

Key Insights

- What you focus on and how you prioritize workstreams will change depending on where you are in the product's life cycle.
- Your goal is to get the product to Iterate & Hone as cost-effectively and quickly as possible, without sacrificing customer value.
- Make sure you and your stakeholders know and agree about the current product life cycle status.

Resources

Each of the product phases has its own complexities and shortcuts. Our next book aims to move you beyond the first 90 days to work through the broader life cycle phases one by one. Keep an eye out for it and check the Appendix to send us content requests. For now, here are three starter resources for the sometimes disorienting early days as a PM:

1. *The Design Sprint* by Banfield, Lobardo, and Wax[3]
2. *Sprint* by Jake Knapp[4]
3. Asana's "Managing the Product Development Process" – Asana is a project management tool. If the link is not active, search for Asana resources https://asana.com/resources/product-development-process (accessed July 2023)

Notes

1. Source: https://commons.wikimedia.org/wiki/File:Sherpas_on _the_Trail_Nearing_Lobuche,_Nepal.jpg (Photographer: Niklas James Sletteland).

2. Kalaignanam, K., K. R. Tuli, T. Kushwaha, L. Lee, and D. Gal. 2021. "Marketing agility: The concept, antecedents, and a research agenda." *Journal of Marketing* 85 (1): 35–58. https://doi .org/10.1177/0022242920952760.
3. Banfield, Richard, C. Todd Lombardo, and Trace Wax. 2015. *Design sprint: A practical guidebook for building great digital products*. First edition. Sebastopol, CA: O'Reilly Media.
4. Knapp, Jake, John Zeratsky, and Braden Kowitz. 2016. *Sprint: How to solve big problems and test new ideas in just five days*. First Simon & Schuster hardcover edition. New York: Simon & Schuster.

Note Taking Page

Chapter 6

Tech Development Processes

Though seemingly isolated between the North Atlantic and
Greenland Sea, Iceland in fact delivers many wonders, including the

DOI: 10.4324/9781003582892-6

Seljalandsfoss waterfall. A product manager's journey through processes is sometimes isolating, despite its interaction with dozens of people. It requires drive and determination to move everyone past difficult setbacks and finally reach an intended positive outcome. For software PMs, this often involves navigating technical development processes such as waterfall and agile.[1]

Playing the Wrong Sport

Jose had worked months to prepare for a stage gate meeting, at which senior management across functions would allow or deny his product to make the next step in the build phase. At the meeting, however, different teams asked unrelated questions. It became obvious that few were following the stage gate process that defines what to look for in product readiness at which stage. In fact, based on the feedback and questions, a different, informal process was still underway. Veterans in the company that Jose had built relationships with told him frankly – this is how things had always been done at the company. Rather than continue to work weekends to meet stage gate meetings, Jose instead worked individually with stakeholders to gain approvals. He was then able to purchase inventory, appear on the price list, and move forward with other steps traditionally kicked off in stage gates. Recognizing which process, or lack thereof, was truly guiding product decisions, Jose was astute enough to successfully realize his product roadmap.

Working Both Angles

For 25 years, a large global company had produced its software in regular releases, one time a year. Minor releases were brought to market a few times in addition. When Mila joined as the product manager, she had to determine how to deliver products faster based on the new software-as-a-service product she knew they had to produce to stay competitive. Rather than try to change the entire organization to an agile methodology, she started by working with engineering to develop agile roadmaps. Over time, the team better understood from these roadmaps what features were needed faster, and they helped advocate for a broader change in year two. Meanwhile, Mila simply updated both waterfall and agile roadmaps to keep both executive and customer stakeholders happy, while keeping engineering on a productive and iterative path.

Scaling with the Company Growth

An early stage start-up was building a SaaS app for marketeers. Sketching out an agile roadmap helped prioritize the limited engineering bandwidth available. Sprints were handled in 2 weeks, with the cofounders serving as product managers to make rapid trade-off decisions. When the company received new funding, it hired an offshore development team to take over and apply two different development teams to vastly expedite product delivery. The agile method was maintained, but scaled. The transparency and flexibility of the agile roadmap allowed the cofounders to remain involved as subject matter experts, while empowering a newly hired product manager to take the reins and welcome new user feedback.

Technology Product Processes

If you're a product manager for a tech company, there are two major development categories you'll likely run into: waterfall and agile. Sometimes you'll see a combination of the two. And of course, like everything in tech, we expect another trending process to show up down the road.

Here we cover a brief summary of waterfall and agile to get you started. It helps to know what you're walking into! Each has its own hurdles and behaviors to expect, and deciphering these early can help you better plan and succeed in getting your product out the proverbial door.

Note: When we talk about processes and the environment surrounding product management in this chapter, we are not describing it as what we think it *should be*, but rather, as it often is today. The goal is for you to be up and running quickly, not to judge which is the best process for a particular product type.

As with most humans, there is often a mix-up between how a process is talked about and what it really is. In many waterfall-led companies, the people you work with may still talk in terms of sprints, agile, and rapid prototyping, which are actually agile methods (see later). In your people interviews and knowledge store reviews (the next chapters), start sifting out the reality of your processes from how they are positioned in conversations, to help keep everyone on track.

Waterfall Product Development Process

If you see wording like *stage gates* and *gatekeepers* and spreadsheets full of *checklists*, you are most likely in a waterfall world, which uses the Waterfall model first proposed by Dr Winston W. Royce in the 1970s. This means that product investment decisions and events happen after specific "mile-markers" in a project development process. Think of it as a linear mapped development process, as we detail more in Chapter 7.

For example:

After each stage in this process, people called "gate-keepers" hold a gate meeting and decide if the project can proceed or not depending on the outcomes from the previous stage.

- If the outcomes meet expectations, the project moves on and receives continued investment.
- If the outcomes do not meet expectations, the project can be recycled back to the beginning of the stage or in some cases canceled altogether.

In practice, it's very hard for companies (especially large ones) entrenched in a waterfall process to cancel development projects once they've started. Because many companies operate on annual budgets, the annual investment has already been set aside, and the project is often completely funded for the year regardless of if it is expected to pass gates or not. It's tough to reallocate funding once it's set, and more often than not, projects keep limping along, even if they are not meeting gate expectations or desired outcomes. You're smart enough to

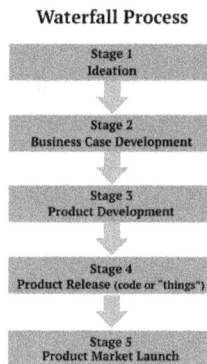

Waterfall Process

Stage 1
Ideation

Stage 2
Business Case Development

Stage 3
Product Development

Stage 4
Product Release (code or "things")

Stage 5
Product Market Launch

A product delivered with a waterfall process follows cascading stages as shown, "falling" from the first ideation stage all the way through to market launch.

be reading this handy guide, so you, at least, won't be surprised if you run into this!

Maybe you've been fortunate to be at a company that *does* cancel projects when they don't meet desired business outcomes. If so, rejoice! Don't let your product enthusiasm interpret a cancellation as a negative. It's a fantastic place to be when a company or organization can say no to draining business choices and overcome the gravitational pull of the "sunk cost fallacy." Start-ups, for example, may change roadmaps quarterly to adjust to customers and the company's venture funding cycle, while large corporations ("corporates") may hold quarterly or first and second half reviews that align to public market stock impact. Understanding how your product process ties to and impacts business outcomes only makes you all the more savvier at getting the customer-loved product to market.

Agile Product Development Process

On the flip side, if you see and hear terms like *sprint, scrum master, stand up meeting, iteration, backlog,* and *sprint review,* you are probably working in an agile world. An agile process is often used when developing software, but the terminology and philosophy of making and creating a minimum viable product (MVP) are making inroads into the physical product space as well. Think of an agile roadmap as showing high-level outcomes, not necessarily linear, as we detail in Chapter 7.

In the agile world, small development teams work on small pieces of the product over short durations called "sprints." Much of the early-stage sprints in start-ups are oriented toward delivering the MVP. This helps the company prove concepts and gain further funding. Later-stage sprints orient toward ongoing user feedback to drive scale or user retention. In larger companies, sprints can denote larger engineering efforts broken up into smaller parts to deliver customer impact faster.

Like many words and terms, agile is often misconstrued and applied to something very different. One challenge? The false notion that you can change product direction every day! One day you are making a heart rate monitor, and the next day you are making a pool chemical cleaner. We are agile! Well, no.

Agile means you review against the product plan often and adjust it in small increments. It does not mean you change the overall product plan at every review.

Action Steps

In your first 90 days, go through the following steps:

1. Find the documentation that defines your new product development process. Key things to understand:
    a. What kind of process are you in? Waterfall? Agile? Hybrid?
    b. How is the process initiated? Who initiates?
    c. How is your project funded? Where/what are the funding source(s)?
    d. Is there a competition for funding? Will you be going up against other products? If so, how are "winners" decided?
    e. Is there an annual cycle to the process or is it done ad hoc based on need?
    f. Who controls the process and how can you influence them?
    g. Are there parallel processes (e.g. Go-To-Market) that you need to be aware of? What else is in place to fund and support building and selling of your product?

Key Insights

- Most companies have product delivery processes in place, but these may or may not serve your primary goals as a product manager – to build and sell great products that customers love. Choose wisely. Invest your energy into processes that truly impact your highest priority goals.
- Know your processes well enough to understand the minimum requirements that move your products through required systems. Avoid the traps of trying to fix all processes or getting drowned by all processes.
- If there is simply no way to deliver your product within existing processes, consider what informal decision trees exist. If those also don't work, leverage your management chain and others impacted to influence how roadblocks can be removed or minimized over time. Meanwhile, get creative to make sure deadlines are met and the top features are included despite process challenges.
- Work processes are not perfect, and there will always be many things that can improve. Influence and change where and when you can. Know what is "good enough" versus what directly impacts success.

Resources

To begin planning how to shape your technical resources, consider leveraging product management software vendor sites. These often provide digital templates, practical ideas, and access to communities.

Digital content changes rapidly. If these links are outdated, search for Product Management Software. To get you started, here are three useful resources:

https://www.productplan.com/explore/

https://www.aha.io/roadmapping/guide

https://www.productboard.com/what-is-product-management/#six

Note

1. Credit: Diego Delso, CC BY-SA 4.0, https://en.wikipedia
   .org/wiki/Seljalandsfoss#/media/File:Seljalandsfoss,_Su%C3
   %B0urland,_Islandia,_2014-08-16,_DD_201-203_HDR.JPG.

Note Taking Page

Chapter 7

Tools

Drones in Sicilian caves help map and harvest data from a vast underground terrain, some of which is inaccessible to humans. Product managers have a range of traditional and modern tools. These not only harvest data, but can expedite, clarify, and enrich the work of taking product concepts to commercialization.[1]

DOI: 10.4324/9781003582892-7

Promises, Promises

A large multinational company held an event with five of its major customers as part of its quarterly collaboration process. The PM presented a roadmap implying a particular version of software (HTML x.x) would be used for the product's administrator management dashboard. At the next quarterly event, two customers were furious when the same roadmap was displayed with a different flavor of the software (HTML x.y), meaning the product would be incompatible with their other tools and even worse, create a regulatory noncompliance issue. The PM could have handled things differently to better manage customer expectations. A roadmap icon that clarified the feature was only tentative, such as Concept or Considering, could have been used instead of the Committed icon. Alternatively, the PM could have decided not to share roadmaps at these events and instead lead a workshop on customer needs and why those needs were essential (e.g. cross-tool compatibility, security compliance). The roadmap can be a helpful tool, but only if used in context of how it will affect its user.

Weighing the Decision

A PM was at a crossroads. If they merged multiple product modules into one platform, it would simplify product delivery and make R&D sprints more impactful. At the same time, forcing customers to buy an entire platform instead of a single product could delay sales. To make this decision, the PM used multiple tools, including a pro/con list, a voice of customer survey, a pricing quadrant map, and a weighted view of all requested features that customers would pay for. Together with socializing the ideas among stakeholders for discussion, the tools helped clarify thinking and enabled more articulate communication to finally reach a measured decision. While no decision would be devoid of risk, the measured approach removed some concerns and also united the team around a common understanding.

Finding Better Solutions

It had been 10 years since a company's refrigeration product set was significantly changed. As a known brand name with repeat customers, the company's R&D team simply iterated on known designs and delivered to customer feature requests. The new incoming PM reviewed the market landscape and noticed several trends changing how one could view refrigeration. Taking a few ideas already tossing around in their brain, the PM used ChatGPT (an "over the counter" AI tool) to refine them. Prompts like "how could a refrigerator talk to a truck" and "what's the best way to cool plant-based foods" brought back not only some silly ideas, but also some connections a human might not have thought about. As the teams met for planning new products, the PM had a healthy collection of starting points that sparked excitement among company veterans. The fact the ideas came from artificial intelligence also tempered the major egos in the room as an "objective" source of ideas.

Scaling to Deliver

By now you're familiar with the essential product life stages and processes. The next step is deciphering which tools and methodologies can simplify and accelerate your work. This chapter curates a selection of tools aligned with your latest objective, while emphasizing an essential element – your product roadmap. Your tools may or may not include flying drones, but some AI-led solutions and SaaS tools will definitely take you places you might not reach on your own.

Artificial Intelligence for Product Management

Speaking of artificial intelligence (AI), we would be remiss not to call it out based on the level of visibility it has gained recently (despite its existence for quite a number of years). It isn't exactly a "tool" in the way a framework or a fully packaged app could be categorized. Yet it's by far an essential part of your product management work as you augment your abilities to gain speed to market. We like to think of it like other important resources, like the human kind, yet far more powerful and fast (with no bio breaks). As you attempt to scale, it's typical to assess workloads and goals and hire people to execute.

From one perspective, this is where AI fits in as well. It's a resource.

That said, the capabilities of AI and synthetic brains are far beyond what mere humans can dream up or execute. The most important recommendation we can make here is to greatly consider the effects of what you are doing. AI will do anything. It just *doesn't actually know what it is doing, at least not consciously. It's up to us humans to provide integrity, oversight and a heavy dose of ethics to ensure the tools augment the humans, rather than the other way around.*

As a basic example, if you're using AI to fetch and summarize customer lists, do you have rights to that customer information? Are you using the data according to legal requirements?

You may know the term *priming* from your college psychology class, but it's even more powerful when paired with AI. In priming, you influence how the subconscious acts or makes decisions. Marketing and advertising teams know this well, shaping brand awareness and art and design to pepper possibilities for a consumer's later recall and behavior change.

As a product manager, you're equally susceptible to priming. If you're using AI, you might walk straight into what the

AI has already decided for you. How we even approach our prompts can either add or subtract from the problems of AI. Did you ask for "how to hack an insulin pump" or did you ask for "making a medical device resilient?". Each of the subsequent responses may be altered by your prior prompts. It's up to you to think of alternative prompts or to use different ML models with different contextualization.

As a more nuanced example, if you're using AI to summarize existing research as you conceptualize a new medical product, what human checkpoints have you ensured are built into your work process, to avoid bias, poisonous information and outright harmful information?

Search up "priming in advertising" if you want to more deeply understand what happens with priming. We recommend this video, if still active at the time of publishing:

Tricking Advertisers With Adverts | MIND CONTROL | Derren Brown: https://youtu.be/43Mw-f6vIbo.

In the "Action Steps" section in this chapter, we included a few prompts to help you think about building integrity and trust into the research you're relying on to create your product.

As you rush to deploy the latest and greatest, we greatly urge you to include human oversight and common sense checks. By all means, use AI to augment and expedite your design process,[2,3] *but deploy critical thinking and a moral compass in far greater doses.*

Here are a few examples that reflect what to consider about the use of AI for product management:

- Check that AI has not automatically incorporated data errors or misinterpretations – this is especially concerning for precision engineering products such as buildings, airplanes, and industrial facilities. Ensure your experienced engineers review all proposed specifications, especially those for safety and compliance. Learn to ask repeatedly and document your questions on these important topics, to underscore their importance across the team. Wherever possible, test, then test again, to see how your product works under varying conditions recommended by the AI-researched information.

■ Create opportunities for humans to approve, deny, or support. Acting as a customer, give multiple opportunities to talk to a human/ombudsman for issues (e.g. a traveler stuck at an airport because digital workflows won't allow them to change a flight between two different airline systems). Other oversight possibilities could include reviewing AI-generated proposals for major clients and automated supplier payment systems, as well as visual inspections of end products, walk-throughs of manufacturing sites, and human product testing.

■ Build products that work for more segments. While it's natural to target and build for buying customers, consider where AI is introducing biases because it trained only on one demographic segment. Democratize your product by finding better data sets.

■ Give credit where credit is due. AI can plagiarize copyrighted materials and disregard citations. Run your formal documents through fact checkers, especially if sharing with customers and external entities such as compliance boards and regulatory boards.

Understanding your responsibility for safeguarding its use, there are multiple ways AI can be applied to product management. These include:

■ Mastering prompts to brainstorm new product concepts
■ Capturing novel product requirements from collaboration tools like Slack
■ Layering in scenarios to probe forother ways they could be changed
■ Summarizing articles as you assess market status

- Comparing data tables or instructions to quickly find anomolies
- Drafting product documentation
- Identifying trends or changes in your user base
- Creating customer surveys
- Writing basic blogs

As we write this (without AI support), the technology continues to teach itself and enjoy a boom cycle. For this area, you'll have to always keep an eye out for what's current. Or reach out to the authors for discussion.

Roadmaps – The PM Bible

If there is one tool that is critical to your function, it is the roadmap. This document (or presentation or online diagram or SaaS app) shows when products will be ready, but it's far more than that. Throughout this book, we point to how PMs are the jugglers and multitaskers across many functions, and the roadmap is the centerpiece festival (the Coachella music festival) of all aspects. You'll need to carefully manage and diplomatically communicate the role, status, and usage of roadmaps in your organization. In some cases, you may even be the person introducing the usage of roadmaps.

The roadmap is a vetting tool across your organization to prioritize and either commit, or make notice of, where R&D will spend cycles. It's extremely helpful for communicating timing and status on products and their features. See Figures 7.1, 7.2, and 7.3 for some roadmap examples. Notice the difference between roadmap types depending on what type of technical process your company might be using (see Chapter 6).

Head's up! For customers, a roadmap can sometimes be considered a legal commitment or warranty about what the company ("vendor") will deliver. This is why it's critical to understand the many dimensions of a roadmap and ask careful questions when someone asks for it. In addition, it may be worthwhile to maintain and track external and internal roadmaps that serve the needs of various stakeholders. For example, Sales may want to know what product features are coming and may share this information with customers, but R&D may want to know what specific features to build and how to plan project teams.

Both are important, but the amount of detail shown on each roadmap will vary significantly. Organizations typically carefully manage different versions of roadmaps that have different content on each.

Waterfall Roadmap

Let's take a look at common elements in a traditional waterfall process roadmap that help you create or edit a roadmap.

- A *legend* is usually critical if the roadmap is used in public or with any customer. Distinguish between what is "committed" as something engineering will definitely work on, and what is simply a notion with no teams or funding behind it. You might call this "concept." Remember which roadmap you shared with which customer, since it can be considered a legal warranty in some states ("I thought you said the next version came with a coffee maker?").
- Adding *themes* is helpful if your collection of features in the roadmap is meeting a particular need. Maybe it's "speed of service" for your next networking device, or "comfort" for your latest armchair designs. Themes help convey value beyond a feature list.
- *Timeline.* This can be weeks, months, quarters, or years, depending on your company culture, type of

development process, and type of product. Hopefully by now you realize why we emphasized product types in Chapter 1. Software products may have new versions every 2 weeks. Cars may come out annually. Buildings, well, that could be a few years.

◼ *Versions.* Every company has a way of naming product versions, from one delivery to the next. It could be linear numbers like models 120, 130, and 140. It might be constellation names or rock bands. Or if it's an existing product line, an addition to the prior name, like Apollo I and Apollo II. It's essential you keep your version terminology consistent, since many workflows cue off this number or name. In software products, you definitely want a clear version number in case of security patching or debugging tracking. It's OK if it looks like a serial number! 2023.21.3.4.1 is important if only the .1 at the end has a security vulnerability and .2 does not.

◼ *Date.* Simple, yet super helpful. Features in different products are obsolete at different paces. Your orthodontic product might be dramatically changing every month, meaning the prior month's roadmap is probably already out of date. Customers awaiting the purple fur-lined braces package by February will be disappointed if they accidentally find and rely on an obsolete roadmap. Keep your roadmap publish date front and center to know what's current.

Figure 7.1 is a simple illustration of a life cycle roadmap using the Waterfall process. The boxes below the orange Product Lifecycle Process articulate how this particular organization defines its product process, from Ideas all the way to End of Life (EOL). The G1, G2, etc. represent the Gates a product must pass to reach the next phase of the process. The arrows below the gates call out some of the major teams involved in this particular product's phases, including Product

Development, Product Marketing, and Sales, in addition to the primary R&D and PM teams.

Agile Roadmap

Now let's look at companies that iterate quickly, often with products like mobile phone game apps or SaaS applications. Roadmaps in these organizations provide a high level view of where a product needs to go, not necessarily the exact time and nature of each version or feature's delivery. They may spell out the different team names available to work on features and the different parts of the product like the platform, mobile, or web versions (remember Chapter 2).

The main benefit of an agile roadmap is its flexibility. Teams can see what is on the overall vision, then each team chips away at their part, changing monthly or quarterly based on customer feedback and the PM's guidance. Other mechanisms that are part of the agile methodology pick up where the roadmap leaves off.

Here's one agile example to help you visualize how ideas are broken down into sprints:

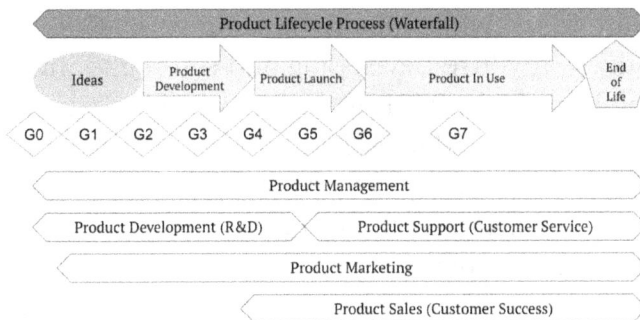

Figure 7.1   Example – lifecycle roadmap, waterfall.

The following example shows itemization by development teams managing different parts of the product, like the IT and Platform components:

We selected both of these examples to also point you to fast-changing (agile?!) vendor blogs that we cited in the "Resources" section in Chapter 6. While they typically prime you by overemphasizing the use of their particular SaaS tool, they are still useful in your first 90 days. You'll want to use select resources to dive deeper on certain topics that we cover only briefly in this get-up-and-running handbook.

When Do You Need a Roadmap?

Early stage start-ups may need a minimum viable product (MVP) far before they need a full-on roadmap. How do they build without a roadmap? They leverage their strong connections with just a few customers or customer types. MVPs can be sketched out and jointly developed alongside these customers, who can also serve as beta testers. A prototype prompts important feedback and moves toward development iteratively. If you're still determining the customer problem to solve, how to go about solving it, and what to build, a roadmap may be too advanced. It might be enough to keep a running list of future feature ideas, while rapidly building your MVP.

Alternatively, if you're developing and starting to invest in engineering beyond the MVP, a roadmap will be extremely useful to guide R&D and keep all the work streams and groups aligned. You may also be required to have a roadmap to earn financial backing (funding) for your idea.

For any larger organization, a roadmap is almost always necessary. There could be multiple engineering teams. They could be dispersed geographically. And simply keeping internal teams informed is far more efficient with a refined "source of truth" roadmap.

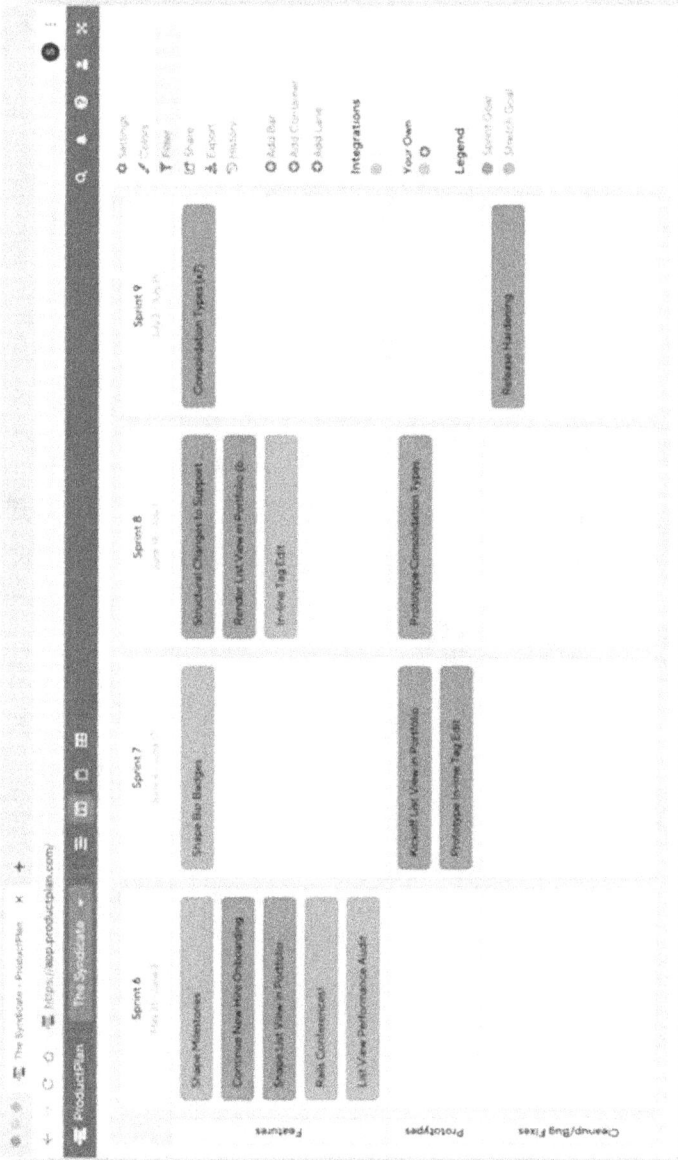

Figure 7.2 Example – sprint "roadmap." Source: https://www.productplan.com/learn/agile-roadmapping -process/.

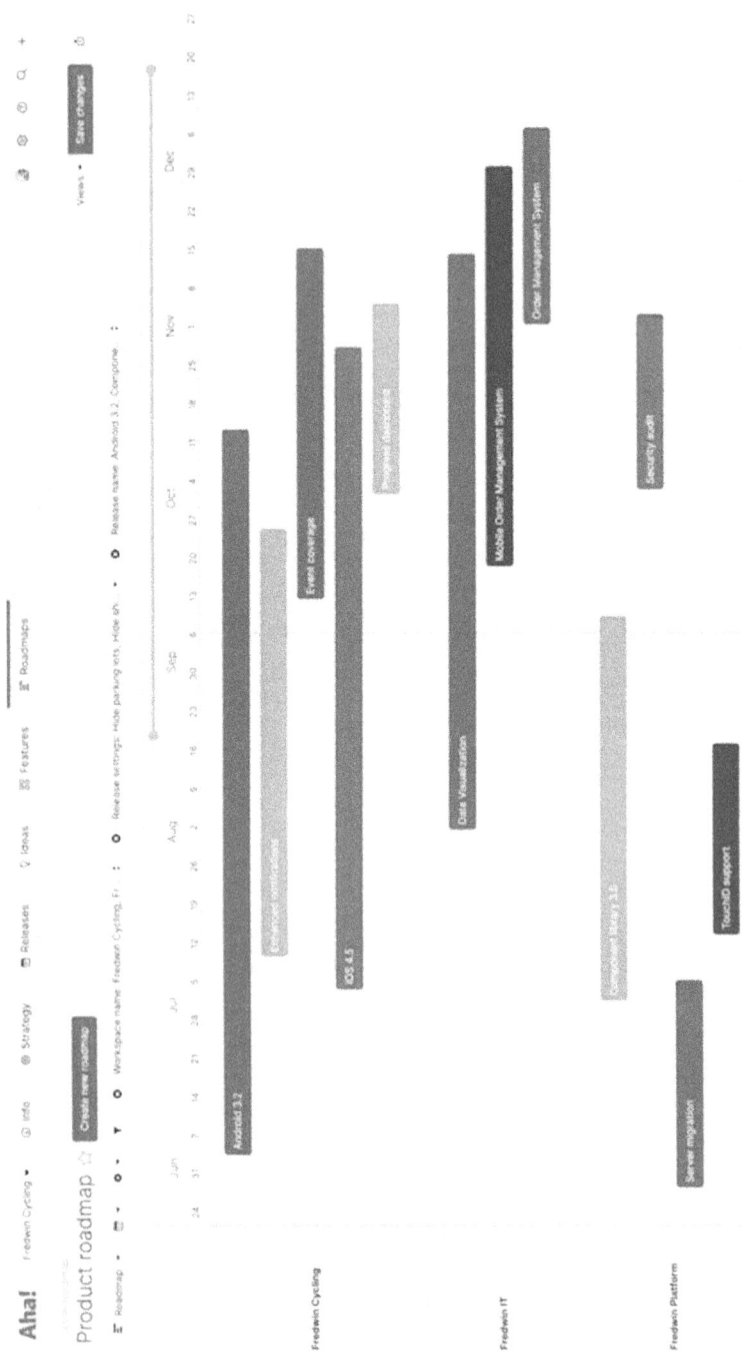

Figure 7.3 Example – developer team assignments. Source: https://www.aha.io/roadmapping/guide/product -roadmap/how-do-product-managers-build-an-agile-roadmap.

Since we're in the tools chapter, here's another roadmap example, from Aha!, a company that makes product management software. Automating roadmap tracking and saving everything in the cloud can help tremendously to keep yourself sane:

Figure 7.4 shows a sample product roadmap from a software subscription you can buy to manage products. This example shows a timeline for product delivery, and various swimlanes for different product types, as a simple example template. Interactive solutions from various providers can simplify product feature tracking and rapidly produce helpful roadmaps.

Action Steps

In your first 90 days, step through the following:
1. Map out your tool inventory by product phase – use the template in this chapter's Resources section and talk to other PMs at the company (if any)
   a. Are there tools that you didn't expect to find and if so, what are they for?
2. Define the gaps
   a. Review the tools you have and compare against the table provided. Where are the gaps in your toolbox? What is missing?
3. Use your tools!
   a. Update any outdated information (e.g. business case, market sizing, etc.)
   b. Review the tool inputs with key stakeholders
4. Try AI
   a. If none of the above include AI-assisted or led tools, make sure you try ChatGPT or similar prompt-led technologies.

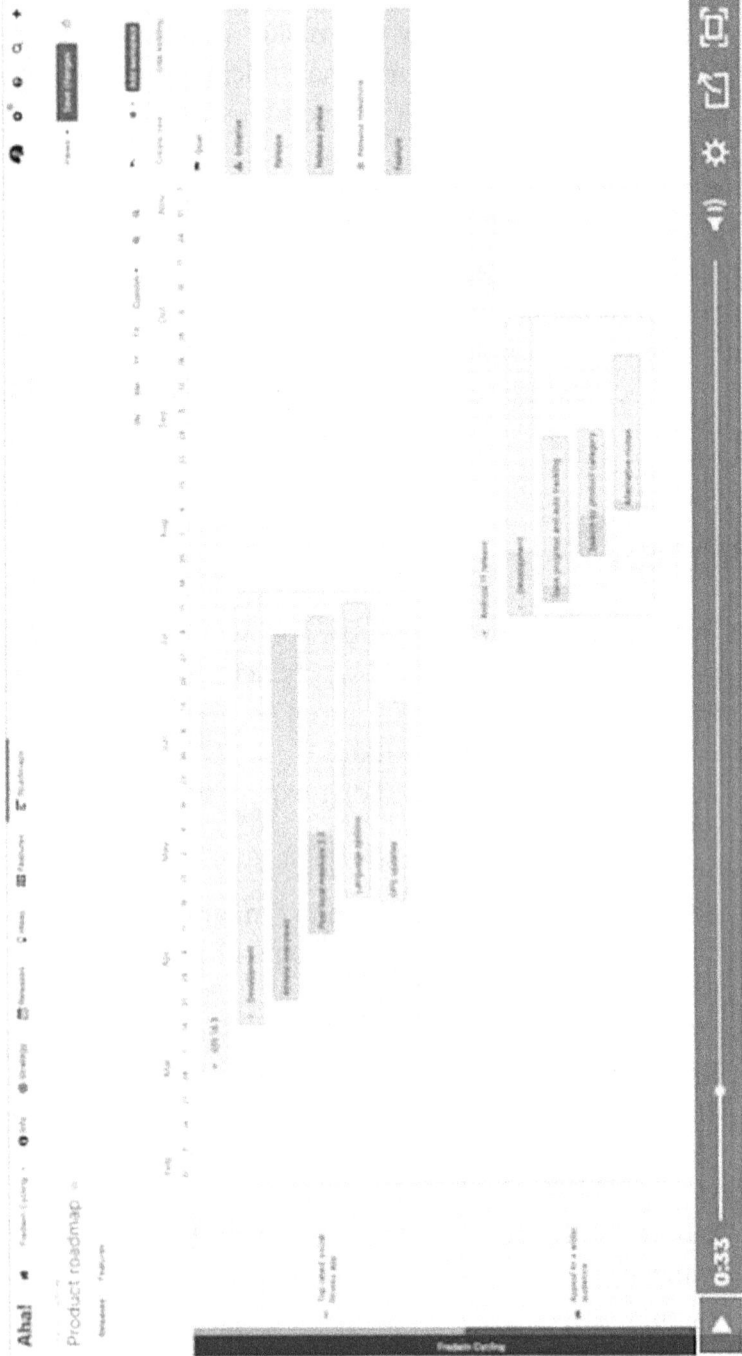

Figure 7.4 Example – product roadmap, software subscription. Source: Aha!.

b. Watch this video to understand how priming affects you as a researcher, and your product users as customers:
   i. https://youtu.be/43Mw-f6vIbo
c. Review the "priming section" and follow-on questions in this chapter. Did these help you improve the information you used? Did they improve the proposed customer experience by balancing AI-led and human-led ideas?
d. If you automated workflows and processes throughout your product, what happens if something goes wrong? Who is accountable? How can the customer have a human to talk to?

5. Double check your research is setting you up well:
   a. Is your product research only from one country, one customer segment, or one well-funded group?
   b. Did you seek out alternative views that might find faults in your current product approach that you had not thought about?
   c. What organizations paid for the research you are building upon? Do they have a vested interest in a different or same outcome of that research? How could this affect your product's success?
   d. Do you feel intimidated or concerned about citing one approach over another, and if so, why? How could this affect your product's success?

Key Insights

■ Roadmaps and AI are two categories of tool sets that can help you get set up initially, then can be reused throughout your product's life cycle.

- We recommend you use any and all available tools to expedite your work. Delivering products is time-sensitive and often involves a major financial investment. Competitors can outrun you and the company requires returns, which means you have to constantly optimize how you operate. Scaling your massive workloads will take a crisp toolset and optimization at every product stage.
- Think about tools in a broad sense. They don't have to be apps or SaaS. Leverage the many free intellectual works that are out there – from frameworks to grids to checklists to Pinterest diagrams – to simplify, clarify, and expedite your product management work. If you're spending more than one hour creating something, it might be worth checking if a starting point already exists (e.g. in Creative Commons or Canva®).
- AI is applicable to your workloads as a powerful tool, yet requires serious human oversight and critical thinking. Learn how to use it and understand its limitations and nuances. You are ultimately responsible for what you build.
- Bring integrity to your work, to eliminate as much bias, inaccuracy, and unsafe methodology as possible.

Resources

Top 10 Product Management Tools

We have included Table 7.1 with our suggestions for The Top 10 Tools you'll want to use in your first 90 days as a PM. This compilation includes methodologies, SaaS apps, and topics relevant to the stage you're at in your role, but we collectively call them "tools" in hopes you can directly apply them to your work.

It is by no means an all-inclusive list. We edited down our far, far longer version for this first 90 days book based on early

Table 7.1 Table of Top 10 PM Tools

	Tool	Use it to	Product phases	Additional resources
1	Value Proposition	Define *who* your product is for and *what* problem it helps solve for your targeted person	Validate Now, Get Strategic Go-to-Market Iterate & Hone	See classic work from Clayton M. Christensen & team on "Jobs to be Done" to define problems your product solves: https://hbr.org/2016/09/know-your-customers-jobs-to-be-done
		Can also be described as what *outcome* your customer will experience because of your product		Work with marketing strategists for creating and refining value props for varied audiences, e.g. www.thoughtmarketing.com

(Continued)

Table 7.1 (Continued) Table of Top 10 PM Tools

Tool	Use it to	Product phases	Additional resources
	In Sales and Marketing use, also captures why your target customers or audience might purchase your product versus available alternatives as an influential positioning statement		A summary of classic work from Geoffrey Moore for value prop creation for early stage tech, and other useful value prop templates: https://tor.medium.com/these-10 -templates-will-make-you-rethink-how-you -write-value-propositions-a789a528fad2 Have a laugh at how AI creates your product value proposition. Most try to formulaically arrange words (*it does this to do that for this benefit*), yet AI can't understand meaning or the impact of words. Occasionally something useful might turn up, but of course, real humans need to test it and love it: Frase.io Scalenut.com Neuraltext.com

(Continued)

Table 7.1 (Continued) Table of Top 10 PM Tools

	Tool	Use it to	Product phases	Additional resources
Notes:				
2	Customer Journey Map	Understand the customer journey (how they discover, evaluate, buy, etc.) and prioritizing where to focus efforts and invest to make this journey fantastic. Also used to keep cross-teams aligned with efforts that truly impact the customer	Fuzzy Front End, Validate Now	General mapping overview: https://www.nngroup.com/articles/journey-mapping-101/ Digital mapping: https://moz.com/blog/customer-journey-mapping-on-google Work with digital marketing experts and ops teams to access customer tracking data across systems and digital properties (e.g. Google Console®, HubSpot® tracking)

(Continued)

Table 7.1 (Continued) Table of Top 10 PM Tools

	Tool	Use it to	Product phases	Additional resources
Notes:				
3	Competitive Analysis	Evaluate your possible products or solutions against the next best product alternatives that also solve the customer's problem. Also used to determine possible features, messaging, and go-to-market plans	Get Strategic Go-to-Market Hone and Iterate	Competitive messaging, live and historical: www.discerna.ai Market analyst reports per industry, e.g. www.IDC.com

(Continued)

Table 7.1 (Continued) Table of Top 10 PM Tools

	Tool	Use it to	Product phases	Additional resources
Notes:				
4	Market Sizing	Determine business model and monetization strategies based on what number of players and pricing the market can bear	Validate Now, Get Strategic Iterate & Hone	Search SEC for market player financials in tax filings: 10-K (US) 20-F (non-US) https://www.sec.gov/ How to read these docs: https://www.investor.gov/introduction-investing/getting-started/researching-investments/using-edgar-research-investments Industry-specific market analyst data, e.g. S&P Global, IHS Market, Forrester Data form industry or product-specific organizations: National Retail Federation, Bicycle Retailer, Wine Institute Use AI research interfaces like Perplexity (but double check the data, it is frequently inaccurate, missing key information, or biased by its data pulling sources)

(Continued)

Table 7.1 (Continued) Table of Top 10 PM Tools

	Tool	Use it to	Product phases	Additional resources
5	Financial Analysis	Develop a cost model and budget to demonstrate return for the product development investment (including ongoing maintenance and support costs)	Validate Now, Get Strategic Iterate & Hone	HBR Manager's Guide to Finance and Accounting: https://info.email.online.hbs.edu/finance-accounting-ebook SaaS: https://www.thesaascfo.com/all-saas-models/
Notes:				
6	Roadmap	Map out what features and capabilities will be delivered by R&D when. Public-facing variations are also used for briefing Sales and Customers	Get Strategic When to Stop Iterate & Hone	/projects/4247 Agile example: https://github.com/orgs/github/projects/4247 Waterfall example: https://www.teamgantt.com/waterfall-model-template Roadmap App examples: https://www.aha.io/ https://craft.io/ https://www.productplan.com/ Capture customer requirements from Slack for roadmap planning: https://www.productboard.com/ Product Board
Notes:				

(Continued)

Table 7.1 (Continued) Table of Top 10 PM Tools

	Tool	Use it to	Product phases	Additional resources
Notes:				
7	Project Planning	Expediting and organizing the many tasks for building and selling products	Get Strategic	Classic Project Management Institute templates and tools (some paid and some free): https://www.projectmanagement.com /Templates/ Team management apps: https://asana.com/ https://monday.com/ https://trello.com/ Software management app: https://www.atlassian.com/software/jira
Notes:				
8	Market Sizing	Determine business model and monetization strategies based on what number of players and pricing the market can bear	Validate Now, Get Strategic Iterate & Hone	Search SEC for market player financials in tax filings: 10-K (US) 20-F (non-US)

(Continued)

Table 7.1 (Continued) Table of Top 10 PM Tools

	Tool	Use it to	Product phases	Additional resources
				https://www.sec.gov/ How to read these docs: https://www.investor.gov/introduction-investing/getting-started/researching-investments/using-edgar-research-investments Industry-specific market analyst data, e.g. S&P Global, IHS Market, Forrester Dataform industry or product-specific organizations: National Retail Federation, Bicycle Retailer, Wine Institute
Notes:				
9	Risk Management	Evaluating risks to product introduction including market risks, discrete product failure risks, and cybersecurity risks	Get Strategic Iterate & Hone When to Stop	American Society for Quality https://asq.org /quality-resources/fmea FAIR: https://www.fairinstitute.org/

(Continued)

Table 7.1 (Continued) Table of Top 10 PM Tools

	Tool	Use it to	Product phases	Additional resources
Notes:				
10	Business Model	Define how you will make and sell your product to satisfy stakeholders (customers, investors, channel partners, etc.)	Get Strategic Iterate & Hone	Business Model Canvas: https://www .strategyzer.com/canvas Business Data Visualization: Tableau® Thought Spot®

Source: © 2024 Taylor & Naunheimer

reviewer feedback. If you love this approach, let us know and we will include the super sized version in our next book. Scenario planning, digital marketing tools, business model generators – there is so much more available to advance your techniques. Check out the Appendix section to share back your favorite tools to include as future resources or to ask us to include other areas.

Our top ten list:

1. Value Proposition
2. Customer Journey Mapping
3. Competitive Analysis
4. Prototyping
5. Market Sizing
6. Financial Analysis
7. Business Model
8. Roadmap
9. Project Planning
10. Risk Management

How to use the Table 7.1:

1 – Jump immediately to the deliverable you're working on now.

Even when you know your product life cycle stage and what type of product, the real-world throws in ad hoc deadlines. If you're suddenly meeting with project sponsors, your value prop and financial analysis might be urgently needed. If you're bringing together teams for an off-site, you'll have to delineate some project management tasks and align on the customer journey. Consider what you need this week and start there.

2 – Understand the entire table.

In your first 90 days, get familiar with all the tools in the top 10. At some point in your product life cycle, every one of these will come into play. As mentioned, you'll need different tools once you've been around a few product versions and portfolios at your company.

3 – Grow.

The table provides a persistent construct for focusing your career development year over year. Each one of these areas can be perpetually honed and continuously improved. Use the empty row underneath each tool to note your own toolsets and organizational resources. Use it with managers and coaches to explore new and better potential methods. Use it with peers to share best practices and "finds" that save you time and effort. Just like craftspeople and apprentices, social situational learning works wonders.[4]

Alternatively, you can experiment with Notion (www.notion .so) to create your own continually updated table resource. Like how we provided you a tool to keep track of your tools?!

It's not the tools per se that will help you succeed. It is using them to practice your craft in the most efficient way possible that will enable you to do more with less.

For a summary of the product phases, see Chapter 5.

Notes

1. Credit: ESA, Natalino Russo, www.natalinorusso.it, CC BY-SA 3.0 IGO, https://www.flickr.com/photos/europeanspaceagency/ albums/72157634951682045/.
2. Verganti, Roberto, Luca Vendraminelli, and Marco Iansiti. 2020. "Innovation and design in the age of artificial intelligence." *Journal of Product Innovation Management* 37 (3): 212–227.
3. Source: Naunheimer & Taylor, 2024.

4. Lave, Jean, and Etienne Wenger. 1991. *Situated learning: Legitimate peripheral participation.* Cambridge: Cambridge University Press.

Note Taking Page

Chapter 8

Skills to Succeed

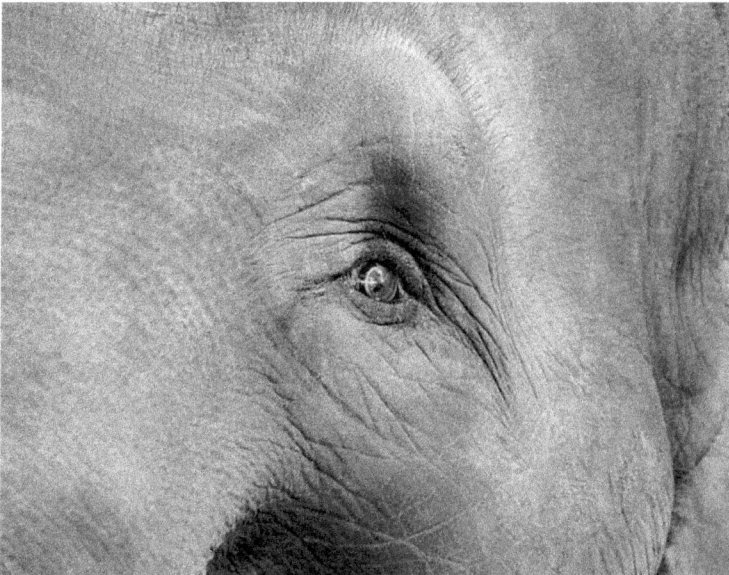

Though commonly recognized for their large size and versatile trunks, elephants possess empathy, social skills, and intelligence. They mourn their dead, use past experiences to inform current decisions, and can recognize themselves in a mirror.[1] Far beyond knowing your product's facts and figures, knowing yourself and your own collection of skills and behaviors can increase your influence and impact. This self-awareness can raise emotional intelligence (EQ), and perpetual development of both IQ and EQ will support your career growth as you lead more products, portfolios, and companies.[2]

DOI: 10.4324/9781003582892-8

Engineered to Win

Ming Ming had been in her product management role for 3 months when a division-wide Operational Review meeting came up. The review findings made clear that customers had been waiting long enough for a particular new feature in her product and soon would migrate to a competitive product rather than continue to wait. Ming Ming went first to her engineering lead and listened carefully. Practically every idea to expedite the missing feature set seemed impossible. If she were to speed up product delivery, it would mean skipping upgrades of key libraries in a related software product – this could leave the product full of vulnerabilities for any hacker to exploit. As she and her engineering lead discussed, there was simply no way to avoid the upgrades leading to the feature delay. Ming Ming quickly developed a key customer list and with Sales, called each one, explaining the situation and why the product timing was designed as such. Once customers understood the quality and security going into the next release, they felt more comfortable waiting and communicating the delay in their own organizations. Ultimately, the skills of listening and analyzing technical trade-offs were essential for Ming Ming to manage her product's success.

Know When to Fold Them

When you can't build a product yourself, outsource! Brad thought it would be a fantastic idea to partner with an independent inventor to bring a new product to market. The product was a completely physical product and from a technology perspective it was leaps and bounds above the performance of the current best-in-class products on the market. The negotiations took a long time (almost 2 years), and it was difficult to trust certain data, but in the end, Brad was convinced that

*bringing this product to market for his company would be
game changing. Once the partner agreements were signed, the
inventor and Brad's company uncovered serious trust issues
when it came to discussing how exactly the product worked.
For Brad to sell it, he had to know all the details so he could
explain performance benefits to customers. But the inventor
was steadfast and refused to "open the box" for review. Brad
had to fund a multimillion-dollar program to build his own test
facility – just to get the data and prove that the product worked.
What started off as a simple exercise to bring in a product from
outside turned into a decade-long engagement that only started
to turn positive cash flow in later years. Trust your observations
and act on them quickly. If you're noticing a lack of collaboration or missing teamwork early on in a business relationship,
consider changing your partnership plans.*

No Blame Games

*Sixteen months into product development for a renewable
energy company customer, the engineering team began to com-
plain. Why were they using this particular code? Why had they
outsourced the event management tool? How come they didn't
include the four authentication mechanisms that engineering
knows how to build? Luckily, Lucy, the extroverted PM, heard
the rumblings. She worked individually with the introverted
key developers to listen, gently reminding them of the past stage
gate. In those prior meetings, engineering had been invited to
comment and advise on roadmap plans. Not a single engineer
shared feedback in those meetings, nor mentioned anything
about the issues they were currently raising. Lucy reflected
whether or not she had provided enough mechanisms and
empathy in the earlier rounds to act on feedback from diverse
groups. Historically before she joined, had engineering even
been asked? Moving forward, Lucy set up anonymous email*

*lists and added three reminder communications and a final
Web-based survey with specifically scoped questions. With these
adjusted approaches, more information flowed from engineering, and the next product iteration was met with less resis-
tance. Using her interpersonal influencing skills and listening
to the new feedback loops, Lucy was able to explain decisions
and show where ideas were or were not incorporated. With no
blame introduced on either side, Lucy found a way to balance
team inclusivity and productivity to move the product through
its life cycle.*

Managing the Mental Game

Our prior chapters focused on actions and information. This
chapter brings in the intangibles – your skills and attitude.

We also speak the unspeakable – product management can
be grueling. For the days you question your life's work decision, we have a bit of motivation as part of this chapter. As
everyone learned through COVID days, managing your mental health coping skills is as important as managing your job
skills. For almost every product manager we work with, there
are days that can feel pointless and isolating, and we want all
of you to know – this is part of it, and you can get through it!
More on that in a moment.

In addition to the work itself, an exceptional amount of
people and analytical skills will be essential for product management success.

For your first 90 days, here are the top three categories
of skills we consider critical. If you need to, hire a coach to
assess and brush up on these skills (and to help with that
isolation we mentioned). No matter what, practice these skills!
Soon enough they'll become embedded.

Top Three Categories of Skills

Emotional Intelligence (EQ)

It turns out that even financially, your academic intelligence (measured by IQ metrics) is actually *less important* for success in life and work than your interpersonal skills. Referred to as EQ, or emotional intelligence, those with higher EQs make on average $29,000 a year more, and another $1,300 in annual pay for every point of EQ they increase.[3] EQ can include skills like having self-awareness, knowing how to self-regulate, showing empathy, and managing through social situations.

Business Acumen

Many a poor product manager has lost to their spreadsheet. Great product managers, on the other hand, are resourceful and grasp what it takes to find solace in the numbers. They might realize that pricing as a subscription will bring in more consistent revenue. Or that eliminating an engineer-loved feature (that customers don't care about) will save a month

EQ Thoughts & Actions

Do I understand myself?	Awareness of Self "I am jealous."	Managing Self "I will learn instead of competing."
Do I understand my environment?	Awareness of Situations "That is his boss and he is nervous"	Manage Relationships "I will help him impress his boss."

Figure 8.1   An overview of emotional intelligence (EQ).[4]

Using EQ & IQ

	IQ: INFORMATION	EQ: EMOTIONS
What I Do	Compute Measure Analyze	Perceive Evaluate Empathize
What I Use	Logic Cognition Intellect Reasoning Analysis	Intuition Creativity Motivation Improvisation Social Skills

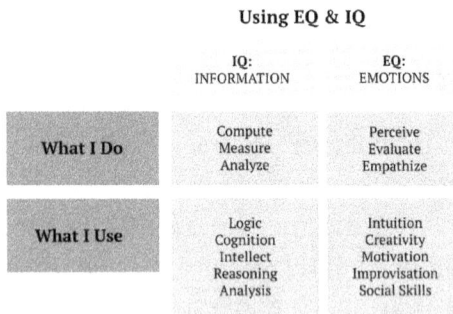

Figure 8.2   An overview of IQ and EQ skills to help evaluate your strengths and weaknesses.[5]

and $120,000. A strong business sense helps right the ship and streamline decision-making. We describe this as business acumen. In short, it means the ability to manage finances while you're creating and building and selling.

Communication

Though it also takes emotional intelligence, we call out communication separately because we know this skill is a make or break factor for PMs. A stellar PM can work with very different personality types, influence without authority, defuse situations, and excite teams to rally around a goal. All of this takes exceptional communication skills. For those in tech, communication is ranked as "one of the prime characteristics required by employers in the engineering industry."[6] At least 40% of our time at work involves communicating, whether role-specific tasks like we outlined in prior chapters, or managing emails, searching and gathering information, or communicating and collaborating internally.[7]

Reading and answering e-mail	28
Searching and gathering information	19
Communicating and collaborating internally	14
Role-specific tasks	39
Total	**100**

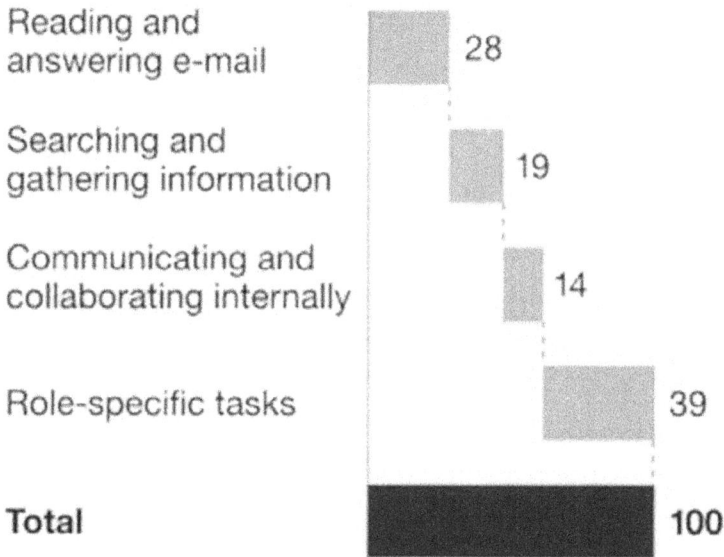

Figure 8.3   Time spent on work communications, by type.[8]

The PM Next Door

If you ask coworkers (like we did) about what makes a great product manager, a few more key skills repeatedly come up. We'll mention them here. We'll also ask you for your input – see the Appendix later to email us.

Decision-Making

Product decisions come up frequently and are multifaceted. As good fortune has it, many of them come with a tight time frame and plenty of discord (note the sarcasm). A great PM listens carefully to the situation, then knows how to analyze the inputs for a measured path forward. This includes documenting and communicating why decisions are made. It also includes leaving heated emotions aside to always consider what is absolutely critical to make and sell the product. Eye on the prize! Part of decision- making also involves knowing who might have to make the decision when it's not you. GMs, CEOs, and others have to make the highest stakes decisions, and great PMs know how to tee up information and perspectives to enable sound decision-making.

Collaboration

If you can get along with dolphins and sharks, and leopards and snails, chances are you know how to work across your PM stakeholders. We define collaboration as making something better by working together with others. It does not mean bulldozing over others or stealing ideas. In the ultimate collaborations, products get more secure as they're more scalable or more intuitive as they're more complex.

Collaborating with different user types and job functions can make your product balanced in a way that's difficult to achieve in your own little missile silo underground. Especially for products that integrate with others or rely on partnerships, there is no substitute for the ability to collaborate.

Stepping Away to Reevaluate

At some point in your first 90 days, it happens to the best of them. You may become completely overwhelmed with the processes and see so much dysfunction that you're ready to hand in that cool company electric car and walk away from your new company-issued Mac. This is the PM's equivalent to product hype cycle's "trough of disillusionment"[9] and almost every product manager will experience it. People may be difficult to access or won't work collaboratively; processes are sometimes incompatible; and the product is not where it needs to be for true market success.

Do not get discouraged! (Well, it's ok to *feel* discouraged, just not to get gridlocked to the point of not taking productive actions.)

Take a moment to decipher if it's just the typical swarm of challenges that any product manager will need to navigate. Or, are there truly obstacles that no matter how much you invest, influence, advocate, and lead, will never get worked around or resolved. Could it be you're still too early in to feel settled?

To collect your thoughts, it can help to focus back on a key tool: your roadmap.

Remind yourself of roadmap status. What were you able to deliver? What progress has been made? What features truly are critical to customer delight?

In large, legacy organizations, it can help to realize the company has been around a while and despite all the apparent dysfunction has still been "successful enough" to keep up with payroll and serve its customers. Look at any products that have made it out the door successfully. Anything you can replicate? Look at excessive costs or waste. Anything you can proactively cut?

In early-stage "fuzzy" ventures, determination and optimism are your best friends. Remember the thousands of "failures" that great inventors experienced before their products became everyday items. Even during the Great Depression, products like the first copy machine, seismography meter, and electric guitar came to life![10] Your steadfast belief in the product might be just the edge the organization needs to push out a solution and a next step forward. Believe.

There will always be problems to solve, and this is the promise and challenge of product management. Your job is never done. Your brilliant communication skills, deeply analytical brain, and ability to work with anyone will get you through. You just need to persist.

Do your challenges sound like any of the stories in this book? Everyone has been there.

That said, if you find it absolutely impossible to perform in your function and have talked through all possible solutions with your management team, it could be time to find an organization that better grasps and embraces best-in-class product management. If that's the case, turn to a trusted career coach or industry contact (yes, you can call us) to move your skills into the right environment. The first 90 days might be too soon to make this evaluation. We just want to call out that managing your emotional well-being and mental health are indeed an important part of the job.

Action Steps

For many areas of skill development, we encourage you to find a partner to hold you accountable to making progress. Immediate feedback loops and different perspectives can vastly speed up your learning. The "Resources" section in this chapter provides some options.

On your own in your first 90 days, you can step through the following:

1. Assess Yourself
    a. Write out your strengths and growth opportunities as they relate to emotional intelligence, business acumen, and communication.
    b. What can you amplify that you really enjoy doing and do well? What do you need to hone so that you can have a minimum level of competence to be successful even if it's not your favorite task/activity?
2. Build a Plan for Skill-Building
    a. For emotional intelligence you might consider:

i. Seeking out diverse personality types and project types that stretch you beyond the typical situations you may have encountered.

1. For example: If you typically work with extroverts, find an introvert. If you have strengths in quantitative assessments, find a qualitative assessment expert to work with. Pay attention to how you react, communicate, and collaborate with these different individuals or groups.

b. For business acumen, consider:

i. Reading through a few public company annual reports and understanding how the profit and loss statement is built.

ii. Talking to your leadership team about what you understand is the current business status of your product and business. Listen to understand how they assess and measure the business.

c. For communication, consider the following dynamics:

i. Global cultures – do you know how to change communications for a colleague in Germany versus India?

1. Consider changing formats, such as using verbal and face-to-face conversations versus sending an email, where tone and intonation can be lost.

2. Learn about what shaking heads, raising thumbs, or other gestures mean in different cultures.

ii. Language – are you getting the outcomes you need or experiencing reactivity and confrontation?

1. Consider reading up on newer nonviolent communications techniques.

a. For example, instead of saying "calm down," ask a question such as, "is there something that is not working for you right now?" Seek

to understand and listen as part of communications, rather than assuming communicating is only a lecture, talk, or quelling of
another's opinion.

2. If there is a technical language barrier such as a
pronunciation issue leading to incomprehension,
be sure to simply ask a person to repeat or type
the words in a chat or send a written follow-up
summary. Say nothing further. It can be offen-
sive to the other if you call direct attention to
their accent or imply some lack of knowledge
or aptitude.

3. Assess Your Organization
   a. Research the culture of the organization. As noted in
      Chapter 3, one way to do this is to have 30-minute
      conversations with colleagues across the organization.
      Aim for 20 or more conversations to really get a wide
      variety of inputs and thoughts.
   b. Write out the key themes of what you heard during
      your research tour. What does the organization do
      well? Where are the opportunities to improve?
   c. Decide how your skills, defined earlier, line up with
      what the organization does well and perhaps where
      the organization can use additional support, and add
      this to your 90-day work plan for accountability.

4. Plan for Ongoing Success
   a. After your 90 days are up, define longer-term actions
      to continue to hone your skills in relation to emotional
      intelligence, business acumen, and communication.
      Some opportunities to consider include:
      i. Evaluating your EQ through standardized testing
         and then addressing some of your opportunities
         to improve (e.g. online test followed by in-person
         coaching).

ii. Part- or full-time advanced education to support building business acumen (e.g. MBA).

iii. Joining an organization (inside or outside of your company) or seeking out a mentor where you have the opportunity to be evaluated on your communication habits and skills in a safe and trust-filled environment (e.g. mentoring opportunity).

Key Insights

■ Emotional intelligence is as important as intellect for success in product management. It helps to balance both, since you'll handle varied types of work – analyzing concrete data like component costs and influencing decisions like negotiated product timelines.

■ Some natural attributes like an analytical mind can map well to the product management role, and some skills can be learned. Assess yourself to know what skills you're missing.

■ Most companies have a professional development plan to help you find opportunities to build more PM capabilities. You can also hire a professional coach to keep you on track weekly and point you to custom resources or people.

■ The complexity and federated nature of the PM job can sometimes leave you feeling overwhelmed, stifled, or exhausted. This happens to the best of them! Leading can mean you're the only one seeing what's possible. Find ways to recharge by meeting with happy customers or finishing a simple task. Work with your manager or trusted coaches to express and clear out what's weighing you down. Read about the failures of many a product manager and remember those products still came to life!

Resources

Self-Development Coaches
- ■ Allison J. Taylor, independent global consultant, B2B technology business success
  - – Helps identify personal strengths, weaknesses, and paths to improve
  - – Helps define career goals, aligned to personal goals
  - – Provides accountability with weekly sessions, to execute on goals
  - – Points to resources and networks, especially in the B2B tech sector
  - – Maps progress and works through career decision points
    - • Product management topical and behavioral learning
    - • Intergenerational work dynamics
    - • Intercultural work dynamics
    - • Job applications, job offers, promotions
    - • People dynamics and real-world interactions
    - • Career changes and transitions
  - – Email: allison@thoughtmarketing.com

Communications Coaches
- ■ Matt Abrahams, independent coach, Stanford Graduate Business School lecturer, author
  - – Helps work through public speaking anxiety and high-stakes presentations
  - – Coaches how to be clear, concise, and confident in Q&A, objection handling, and feedback
  - – Works on stage presence, articulation, concision, and delivery
  - – Email: matt.abrahams@gmail.com

University Career Centers, especially at MBA programs

- Lists of local employers seeking product managers
- Tracking on surveys for different industry skillsets
- Testing for career aptitude

Personality Tests

- Myers Briggs, 7 Circles, Enneagrams, StrengthsFinder Communication & Collaboration Skills
- Book: Matt Abrahams, *Think Faster, Talk Smarter*
- Book: Brian Glaser, *A Curious Mind*
- Book: Mark Ettensohn, *Unmasking Narcissism, A Guide to Understanding the Narcissist in Your Life*
- Listening Tour Management Practice: often used for new managers, but equally effective for people in new roles Consultants
- This book's co-author, Allison J. Taylor

Notes

1. World Animal Protection Organization, https://www.wor ldanimalprotection.org/latest/blogs/elephants-emotions-and -empathy/.
2. Credit: Saya Kresnanta dari Bali, https://medium.com/@_nik- las, CC BY-SA-4.0, https://commons.wikimedia.org/wiki/File :Elephant%27s_Eyes.jpg#filelinks.
3. Source: Travis Bradberry: https://www.forbes.com/sites/travis- bradberry/2014/01/09/emotional-intelligence/?sh=528a457a1ac0.
4. Source: Taylor, 2024.
5. Source: Taylor, 2024.
6. Source: UNESCO International Centre for Engineering Education (UICEE), Faculty of Engineering.
7. Source: McKinsey Global Institute (MGI): The social economy: Unlocking value and productivity through social technologies.

8. Figure Source: McKinsey Global Institute (MGI): The social economy: Unlocking value and productivity through social technologies.
9. Source: https://www.gartner.com/en/research/methodologies/gartner-hype-cycle.
10. Source: Thought Marketing Webinar, https://www.thoughtmarketing.com/webinar-core-leadership-behaviors/.

Note Taking Page

Chapter 9

Next Steps

Planets closer to the sun orbit faster, making Mercury the fastest with an 88-day year. We hope this book has helped you condense time, work faster, and set yourself up well for your first 90 days building and delivering products. Just as this color-enhanced topographical map toward Mercury's northern side reveals, there will be highs and lows in your product management terrain, but that does not mean you can't continue to deliver out-of-this-world products and solutions.[1]

DOI: 10.4324/9781003582892-9

Industry-Specific Product Management

Our goal with this book has been to get you up and running and oriented, for your first 90 days in a new product management role. There is far more to the profession, of course, than what we have documented here. Most notable are industry-specific methodologies you can explore further, especially if you are building mission-critical products like airplanes, healthcare devices, and automobiles. In the tech sector, product managing cyberphysical and Internet of Things (IOT) products deserve additional learning for cybersecurity resilience.[2] In the consumer world, privacy and safety considerations come into play. For today, though, we hope you congratulate yourself for having made it this far!

What Do You Do Now?

As next steps, we recommend you connect with other product managers to compare notes and continue to optimize your tools, processes, and skills. Finding peers in your own industry can also help uncover the industry-specific methodologies we call out above (not to mention managing your emotional well-being).

Finally, we'd like to ask for a few words of feedback. Please hop to the Appendix to send 60-90 seconds worth of feedback to your authors. Why 60-90? That's the ideal time for a traffic light cycle to both encourage walkers and reduce traffic congestion, according to the National Association of City Transportation Officials. If it works for beating traffic, it works for us! Thank you in advance for your comments.

And congratulations on getting yourself to this point. If you have the determination, tenacity, and empathy to teach yourself new techniques with a handbook, your future as a product manager is even brighter than those reflective strips you see driving at night on the highway (another great example of a product manager's success).

Coaching and Consulting

If you or your organization need customized go-to-market support, or real human accountability for individual development, we frequently deliver one-on-one coaching, group workshops, classes, and custom advisory services. Our contact information is noted in the Appendix. We look forward to meeting you (and your products!).

Note

1. Photo source: NASA, PIA16388 NASA/Johns Hopkins University Applied Physics Laboratory/Carnegie Institution of Washington.
2. Khan, Wazir Zada, M. H. Rehman, Hussein Mohammed Zangoti, Muhammad Khalil Afzal, Nasrullah Armi, and Khaled Salah. "Industrial internet of things: Recent advances, enabling technologies and open challenges." *Computers & Electrical Engineering* 81: 106522.

Appendix

Community Contributions

We welcome all feedback and updates for this book covering your first 90 days. Email with the subject line "Book Feedback" to: info@thoughtmarketing.com

For 60-90 seconds of feedback, just answer these questions:

1. What did you find most valuable?
2. What was missing?
3. Will you share this book with others? Why or why not?

Based on early reviewer feedback, we are preparing our second book that walks you through the entire product life cycle process start to finish (pending the volatility of our work schedules). Please share your suggestions and ideas for the next book in email with the subject line "Your Next PM Book – Ideas." We'll make sure to cite you!

Index

Source of truth roadmap, 78
Sprints, 64–65, 69
  roadmap, 77–79
Stage gate process, 60
Stakeholder maps, 36–38
  mind maps, 37–38
  overview, 36–37
  worksheet, 37–38
Subject matter experts (SMEs),
    31, 33
Sunk cost fallacy, 64

T

Tech development processes
  agile product development
      process, 64–65
  new product development
      process, 65
  waterfall product development
      process, *see* Waterfall
      product development
      process
Tools, 81, 83
  artificial intelligence (AI) tools
    applications, 73–74
    ChatGPT, 70
    considerations, 72–73
    priming, 71–72
    recommendations, 71–74
  roadmaps, 83
    agile roadmaps, *see* agile
        roadmaps
    development process, 78–82

icon, 69
overview, 74–75
sample, 81, 82
source of truth roadmap, 78
waterfall roadmaps, 75–77
top 10 tools, 84–95
Trough of disillusionment, 104–105

V

Value of products
  charge for, 18–19
  definition, 16, 17
  for digital-only products, 16
  hypothesis, 25–26
  measurement, 16–17
  price, 17–18
  product label, 19
Value proposition, 26
Voice of customer (VOC), v, 46

W

Waterfall product development
    process, 62–64
  gate-keepers, 63
  stages of, 63
Waterfall roadmaps
  date, 76
  legend, 75
  lifecycle roadmap, 76–77
  themes, 75
  timeline, 75–76
  versions, 76

For Product Safety Concerns and Information please contact our EU
representative GPSR@taylorandfrancis.com
Taylor & Francis Verlag GmbH, Kaufingerstraße 24, 80331 München, Germany

www.ingramcontent.com/pod-product-compliance
Lightning Source LLC
Chambersburg PA
CBHW061321220326
41599CB00026B/4975